M000195930

The Neighbor from Bergen Belsen

Yaakov Barzilai

First Hebrew Publication: Aked, 1997

Translated from the Hebrew by Philip Simpson

25 Hulme Hall Road,
Cheadle Hulme,
Cheshire SK8 6JT, U.K.

Copyright © 2020 Yaakov Barzilai

All rights reserved; No parts of this book may be reproduced
or transmitted in any form or by any means, electronic or
mechanical, including photocopying, recording, taping,
or by any information retrieval system, without the
permission, in writing, of the author.

Tel: 0161-485-5305
Email: prjks@mighty-micro.co.uk

ISBN 978-965-575-235-9

Dedicated To the Survivors
Who were sentenced to life imprisonment with hard
memories and no remission for good behaviour

THE NEIGHBOR
from
BERGEN BELSEN

YAAKOV BARZILAI

FOREWORD

In defiance of all logic – the greater the distance grows, the more acute is the vision. Fifty years on, the pictures are as clear as ever.

Memories too put on skin and sinew.

And here is one man who harnesses horses to the carriage and bids the coachman drive in the opposite direction, to the starting-line: to rock in the cradle, play hide-and-seek in the woods, and on Seder night ask the four questions, and in between times, smear glue on the maths teacher's chair, and scatter salt on the poppy-cakes and apples given as presents on Purim. And if time allows, drink from the fountain of youth before the tap is turned.

"The Neighbor from Bergen Belsen" is the story of a time, from a personal perspective, in which tears of joy and tears of grief flow together to the sea, and angels in white contend with angels in black.

ONE

In the latter days of March in the year 1933 the signal was given for the great thaw. The white coating that had covered the roads began withdrawing to the lower levels and patches of snow turned into sparkling water, streaming into rivers that were tirelessly striving to break free from their narrow channels. The oaks, which had dressed in bridal garments, divested themselves gradually of the white wedding veils, and fresh green shoots were the first to clap their hands in admiration.

My father's workshop in the provincial city of Debrecen, Hungary, was located in our house in the very heart of the conurbation. The many sewing-machines, clattering away in two daily shifts, gave no respite to my mother, labouring in the nearby kitchen, except when the garment workers took their brief meal-breaks. I, spending all my time in the kitchen – in my mother's belly – saw nothing but heard everything: the bubbling of the pans on the stove, the gyrations of the potatoes in the water, dancing to the sounds of the hissing flames beneath them, the whispering of the workers at meal-times, and even the petty squabbles that erupted from time to time between my father and my mother, introducing a little colour into their lives.

My father was reckoned a master craftsman among tailors and an enthusiast for the trade, which he dominated like a monarch in his kingdom. His days were divided between the massive cutting-table, where the materials were heaped in co-lourful profusion, he setting to work with his scissors, tongue lolling from his mouth like the tongue of an excited dog – and his excursions to markets and fairs in far-flung provincial towns, where he used to sell his finished products. Weekends were devoted to his greatest love of all – card-games in the exclusive "Golden Bull" club.

During the second half of March, I began to tire of intern-ment in my mother's womb, and on the 29th I escaped from it. This was the first weekend that my father went without his card-game at the "Golden Bull" – and this gave a great boost to my ego; from my very first appearance on the stage, I felt myself important. My mother was in the seventh heaven when I wetted her night-dress with my first attempts at suck-ling. But most overjoyed at my arrival were my mother's parents, especially Grandpa Lipa, who had to walk with the aid of a stick on account of chronic leg-pains which usually confined him to his home. His love for me knew no bounds. Compared with other babies, he reckoned I was the acme of human creation.

I had a magical influence on him, until one bright day the

miracle happened: he threw away his stick and began hobbling unaided. That very day he commandeered the pram, installed me in its sumptuous interior – naturally, after my mother had packed me in my public-display outfit – and set out with me for my first outing in the streets of the city. The King of England could not have enjoyed such a degree of attention as it seemed I was enjoying, under the care of my personal escort. Every fifty metres he would stop to listen to the crooning chorus of passers-by besotted with me and with the golden curls adorning my head. And if he felt someone or other wasn't joining in the parade of homage to my beauty, he would protest vociferously until he had exacted from the offender the tribute that he considered my due.

My father was the eldest of eight brothers and sisters, unlike my mother, who had only one sister. My father's parents were strict adherents to the Mosaic code, observing virtually all of the commandments, whereas my mother's parents were decidedly secular. My parents, in their turn, were a compromise between their respective parents.

During one of the daily trips with Grandpa Lipa, when I was already sitting up in the pram, as he pushed it along with unabashed delight, two hooligans suddenly appeared, standing in its way in a stubborn and provocative pose, as if about to declare war on Grandpa and me. Grandpa chose to ignore them and attempt to bypass them, but they changed position adroitly and resumed their blockade of my pram's diversionary route. Grandpa flinched for a moment, but recovered himself. He turned to them politely and asked them to stand out of the way. In reply, the pair of hooligans burst into peals of hysterical laughter. At this point Grandpa reckoned that the moment of truth had arrived, and aggression was the only answer. "Out of the way, now!" he shouted at them, and it seemed that the tone of his voice had done the trick; they both began moving aside. My pram was in motion again, and as Grandpa passed the hooligans, one of them poked a leg between his pair of doddery legs. He saw it coming, but too late. He tripped and fell full length on the ground, giving a final shove to the pram, which began racing away in the direction of a busy road. Grandpa lay there helpless, crying out for help, while I sped towards my destiny. A passerby tried to stop the runaway pram, and got a hand to it; not enough to stop it but enough to cause a sudden change of direction, and it veered off towards a row of houses. When my pram crashed into the iron gate of Number 21, I should by rights have flown out and collided with the gate myself, but not so: Grandpa had strapped me so tightly into my harness that I remained sitting up in the pram. This was an early encounter with the angel sent to preserve me from harm. It was also my last outing with Grandpa Lipa; that summer he died an untimely death.

TWO

When the first Allied bombers suddenly appeared, I was lying in an open field, without so much as a hillock to hide behind. I curled up, as only an eleven-year-old child is capable of contracting his limbs to the size of a button, from the viewpoint of a pilot hungry for moving targets in a broad, flat and featureless landscape. That exhausting morning in Austria, in a village near Vienna, several dozens of Jews were working in this sector, dispersed among the beds of onions, now ready to be uprooted and gathered for the markets. At the age of eleven I was the indentured slave of an Austrian farmer, who wore an impressive yellow patch on the lapel of his coat. My corpulent mother was working close by, watching over me. The hum of the bombers' engines was the signal to scatter in search of refuge. Mother told me it was pointless changing position, since every bullet has an address written on it. I lay down beside the onions that I had just picked and prayed that the pilots' bullets would hit them instead of me. I tried to be swallowed up in the ground, becoming an onion seed buried in a vacant hole – but in vain.

Tibi Berger's father was lying a dozen metres from me. He was praying, asking God to signal to the pilots that we were Jews and not to be harmed. Yonah Adler was crouching nearby. He suddenly came up with the idea that we should all stand and wave to the low-flying pilots, as a gesture of friendship.

"Friends," – he said – "don't forget to point to the yellow patch, so they'll easily identify us!"

"Don't even think about it!" – shouted Tibi Berger's father. "The guards will shoot us straightaway. The English might miss, but the Germans won't!"

The bullets whistled above and around me, even hitting the pile of fresh onions, which splattered in all directions. A long trail of gunfire curled across the field, a sight reminiscent of a herd of cattle pissing in a meadow. For a moment it seemed that Yonah Adler was heeding the advice of Berger senior, and would henceforth try to navigate the course of his life between hostile bullets and friendly bullets, avoiding injury from either. All this time my mother was signalling to me, not to budge from my position. Suddenly, without any prior warning, Yonah sprang to his feet and began running back and forth, shouting to the low-flying aircraft swooping over us in waves: "We're Jews! We're Jews! Don't shoot us!"

Mortal dread descended on us all.

Yonah Adler owned a shoe-shop in our town, a large and spacious shop. Display windows were crammed with a rich selection of fashionable styles from the most prestigious man-ufacturers. He was reckoned a fair trader and a genial man. Every box of shoes that was packed, after selection of the suit-able pair, was wrapped in the ribbon of an unaffected smile. In Yonah Adler's shop, every sale of a pair of shoes was seen as the precursor of the sale of the next. Customers were happy to return to Yonah when the first signs of wear appeared.

In the late thirties a wave of anti-Semitism swept our town. Ruffians from the universities gathered in terror-squads, to settle scores with the Jews. Under cover of darkness these squads were deployed at various points in the town, to lie in wait for Jews returning from evening prayers in the three synagogues. When a suitable victim appeared, five or six ruf-fians would emerge from their dark hiding-places to thrash an innocent Jew who wanted only to return to the bosom of his family, having performed his daily duty to God in the synagogue. The ruffians of the terror-squad would disperse, leaving their victim sprawled on the pavement, bruised and bleeding, his hat crushed and tossed into the road.

One short October day in the year 1939, as every other day of the week, Yonah Adler closed his shoe-shop at seven p.m. He took his leave of the sales assistants and set out towards his home, ten minutes walk from the shop. He had barely taken three paces, when he was confronted by a gang of ruf-fians, extending their range and committing acts of terror not only in dark corners but in well-lit streets as well. Yonah was aware of the nightly terror raids, but was surprised to find that the terror had reached his home patch. Yonah Adler was a fit and active man in his early forties, and shrewd enough to make a habit of carrying a knuckle-duster in his pocket. Finding himself surrounded by the five ruffians, he pulled out the knuckle-duster and adopted a defensive pose, one that could easily be converted to attack. When the first assailant approached him, Yonah didn't lose his nerve but landed a hard upper-cut under his chin – hard enough to make a man see stars in the sky on a misty night. Yonah's unexpected move took his attackers by surprise. One of them recovered his wits, stooped, picked up a big stone and hurled it at the display window of the shoe-shop, which shattered with a resounding crash. When Yonah turned to see the extent of the damage, the ruffians pounced on him from behind, beating him savagely, knocking him to the ground and using his battered body as a parade ground for hobnailed boots. As a finale, they flung him through the smashed window, and all the pairs of shoes in the display were smeared with a red dye.

As Yonah was shouting at the aircraft and running back and forth among the heaps of onions, one of the pilots saw that for the first time he was being offered a moving target. At once he signalled to his mates that he was "taking" it. Hungry for combat he swooped on the target and within seconds had eliminated it with a volley of lethal gunfire. Full of holes, Yonah collapsed beside the big heap of onions. I was lying on the other side of that heap, and I remembered my angel, who had again spread his wings above me.

Yonah Adler was "lucky". He rated a burial, courtesy of

Schultz, the Austrian farmer, in a godforsaken patch outside the fence. On the grave-mound there was an inscription, scratched in the soil: "Yonah Adler, 1902-1944, Pellendorf, Austria".

THREE

Father sat in the "Golden Bull" club with three partners and played cards. This was a Sunday, wreathed in mist. The streets seemed to be wrapped in gauze, like a bridal veil perforated with tiny holes. Thin raindrops beat on the asphalt of the pavement. An ideal day for tormented lovers, to whom torments are an elixir of life; a Sunday to inspire poets secluded in garrets, waiting for the Muse to render them fertile.

Father used to look forward to Sunday, because of the cards. The whole week he spent waiting for the moment when he would sit down with his regular partners at table number 10, with its green baize cover. That Sunday, as usual, at 9 o'clock in the morning he left the house, to the constant chagrin of my mother.

The pattern of Sundays in our house was fixed. The Sunday scenario had three protagonists: Father, Mother and I. Every time Father left the house in the morning, he would promise to be back in time for lunch at 1.00, though he knew full well he wouldn't be returning before midnight.

Mother, accepting Father's promise to return at noon, would spread a white cloth on the table, set out plates, cups and cutlery and await Father's return to the bosom of the family, knowing one of the plates on the table was bound to prove superfluous.

And I, knowing my mother was waiting in vain, and he wouldn't be back until late at night, spent every Sunday in a state of readiness, to be sent at 2.00 precisely to the "Golden Bull" to try and fetch Father home, though I knew by heart the conversation that would ensue in the course of six hours of waiting in the club.

And so it was: at 11.00 my mother was sitting by the window, twitching the curtain and abandoning herself to waiting. At 1.30 she would utter a deep sigh and call my sister and me to sit at the table for our lunch. At 2.00 precisely I was called upon to perform my regular duty.

When Father's partners became aware of my arrival, a cloud of irritation would waft over table number 10. With awe and deference I would approach Father and whisper in his ear: "Dad, Mum wants you at home."

"Soon" – he always replied instinctively. "In the meantime, go to the window and see what's happening in the street."

For six whole hours I would be leaning on the window-sill and staring out into the street. The "Golden Bull" club was situated on the main street, and anyone looking through the window could see and feel the rhythm of the city's pulse. On Sunday afternoons the streets were fast asleep. Not long before, the Sunday service at the big Protestant church had ended; its two towers and impressive porch were clearly visible from my vantage point at the window. The street was a void, yawning wearily after the tumult of the working week.

Under my window there was a taxi-rank, with eight stands. I used to amuse myself watching the progress of the taxis and calculating how long it would take the one at the rear to make it to the front, having the pick of prospective passengers. When the driver of the first taxi started his engine, all the others hurried to shuffle their vehicles forward, heaving them manually; on journeys of a few metres, they preferred to conserve their fuel.

Beyond the taxi-rank stretched the tram-lines, running the full length of the main street. Tiring of the idle panorama revealed through the window, a routine chasing its own tail, I turned my back on the sleepy city and sat on a chair under the window. Smoke-rings floated in the air above table number 10; Father was the only one who didn't smoke. The faces of the players were stony and blank. As each hand was played, I tried to figure out who was going to win it, following the flicker of eyelashes, the puckering of foreheads and the quantity of sweat on the face – but almost invariably I failed to spot the victor. Each of the four was a professional; all held higher degrees in the science of the cards, having graduated from the academy of gamesmanship.

Robbie Friedmann, who sat to my father's right, was one of his closest and oldest friends. But in card-games – friendship is one thing and the tactics of the table something else entirely. Robbie used to arrive for the Sunday games in a formal suit, starched shirt with gleaming cuff-links, and a black bow-tie under his chin. He was a virtuoso in the art of dealing. The pieces of coloured cardboard responded to his fingers as obedient puppets respond to their handlers. As the game progressed Father would be desperately hoping for some favours at his hands, but the cards he dealt were no use to Father at all. His genius was evident not only in his own tactical play, but also in his ability to rumble an opponent's strategy and foil it.

Robbie Friedmann was a regular visitor to our house. Despite the "poker-face" that he maintained in the "Golden Bull" – in social gatherings he showed a volatile temperament. His talent for telling juicy stories, laced with piquant humour, was his favourite weapon. Robbie was a confirmed bachelor – but not as a result of any failure on his part. He was a much sought-after guest at virgins' conventions, and an honorary member of the married ladies guild. No one knew how he made his living; he tended to introduce himself as a travelling salesman.

I remember that during one of his visits to our house, my parents told me to say goodnight to our guests. This was the sign that Robbie was about to tell some risqué anecdote, not for my ears. As usual, I raised no objection, said a polite goodnight to all of them, went to my room and strained my ears to hear Robbie's story. They were all urging him to tell them something sensational.

"Whenever I'm a guest in your house," – Robbie began – "I feel completely naked, because you know me inside and out, and you know all my weaknesses: cards, women and the circus. And speaking of circuses… Do you remember the Italian circus that came to town last year? The circus stayed here for six weeks, and I went along three times a week, for a month and a half. I always sat in the front row. If any of you got to see the show, I'm you'll remember Aladdin, the conjuror with the big box and the elderly assistant, who had the grossest thighs you ever saw. She used to twine herself around him during the performance. A peroxide blonde with five or six layers of make-up. If she were to be dug up a hundred and twenty years from now, teams of expert archeologists and anthropologists would have their work cut out excavating the lady's face. Aladdin called his assistant Cissy. I saw the show more than fifteen times and I always sat in the same seat in the front row. Sitting so close to the ring has advantages and drawbacks as well.

"As early as the second performance I'd noticed the way Cissy was winking at me before Aladdin picked himself a victim from the audience, to be put into the box together with the fat assistant. I was afraid Aladdin might have me figured for a candidate too. Not that I minded cooperating, but the idea of spending time with fat Cissy in a closed box didn't appeal to me at all."

You could sense the growing tension among Robbie's audience. All stopped eating, afraid that even the sound of chewing might overpower the nuances of the story.

"At the fourth performance of the circus I breathed a sigh of relief. Fat Cissy had been replaced by a younger assistant, whose voluptuous charms were a delight to behold and fuel for the imagination. From then on, I was praying that Aladdin would pick me out of the audience. When I looked at the box lying in the centre of the ring, I saw the gates of the Garden of Eden, and the new assistant was smiling at me mischievously... It seemed my prayers were answered, as the evening arrived when the conjuror chose me as his victim. Aladdin told the audience he was about to perform an impressive magical feat, and he showed them that his magic box was empty. To the sound of a fanfare from the orchestra, they escorted me to the box. I was feeling electrical charges surging through every part of my body, at the sight of the charms of the conjuror's new assistant. All my senses were on edge at the thought that within a few minutes, she would join me in the box, and the door would be closed on us. Aladdin ushered me into the box. I heard the click as the door closed behind... but the conjuror's assistant stayed outside. I felt cheated. All that electrical tension in my body just faded away.

"Suddenly I heard a wild cackle, that was somehow familiar. Fat Cissy was reclining there in the box, stark naked. In one hand she was holding a strange-looking box. 'Come here, dearie!' – she tried to entice me.

"I was gagging with nausea, seeing all those folds of fat. 'Over my dead body!' I hissed at her. I thought of retreating, but there was nowhere to go.

'Think twice, dearie, before offering me your dead body,' – Cissy chuckled – 'but if you leave me no choice... Do you know what I've got in this little box here?' she added, mysteriously.

'Some of your fake jewellery, I expect!' – I raised my voice, in no mood for guessing-games.

'No, dearie. In this box lives a very hungry creature, a species of cobra…'

'Eh?… What?… No!… No!' I pleaded at the top of my voice, and my body shaking with fear, I fell into Cissy's arms.

"I don't remember how long I was in the box, but it seemed that evening Aladdin's act lasted as long as the Exile in Babylon. That experience of bewitchment was aversion therapy for me, and I haven't set foot inside a circus tent since. I've also been cured of two of my vices simultaneously: women and circuses. All that I have left are the cards!" – Robbie concluded his story, to the applause of his audience.

Here, sitting in the "Golden Bull" club, I was nagged by boredom. At 8 o'clock I went to my father and begged him to come home with me.

"You go on, son, I'll be right behind you," – he replied, not taking his eyes off the cards. At midnight he came home, exhausted, collapsed on the bed and fell asleep at once. Monday morning he woke up, still wearing his Sunday clothes.

FOUR

In the spring of 1944, something strange happened to the old oak tree in our backyard, which for generations had offered shade and shelter to all those in need. One of its branches broke and it seemed to us the tree was bewailing its loss. That same day Hitler's armies invaded Hungary, and swarms of Nazi locusts swept across the land. Father's workshop was not as it had been before. The eyes of his employees flashed with a green tinge of hatred. Their submissive glances changed overnight, becoming imperious and intrusive, piercing the heart and the guts. Their habitual reticence dissolved, and gradually springs of defiance began bubbling in their gullets, initially forming thin rivulets which over time swelled to the dimensions of a surging stream.

Father, who used to radiate energy and resolve, whose authoritative figure hovered above the workers even in his absence, was suddenly brought down to earth, as if both his wings had been broken.

The veteran seamstress Kitty, who could have chaired the

workers' committee, if the workers had wanted a committee, who always addressed my father in the most deferential style, as "most highly esteemed Sir" – suddenly shouted at him, without rising from her seat: "Hey, you, are you listening? We've decided to stay on today in the factory and work overtime so we can sew enough yellow patches for all your clothes, so in the evening you and all your family can walk the streets with smart new badges on your chests. You're going to pay us extra, of course, in return for our special efforts and the longer hours."

As if he were under the influence of a sleeping-potion, Father's senses clouded over on hearing his employee's words.

My mother, busy peeling potatoes in the kitchen, heard what Kitty had to say word for word. As if bitten by a snake she sprang from her place at the sink, and stood in the doorway separating the kitchen from the workshop.

"Kitty, Kitty," – she cried – "did I hear you right?"

Kitty burst into a peal of hysterical-artificial laughter. Regaining control of herself, she sharpened her tongue and said:

"Although everything has to be said to you twice on account of your defective hearing, this time you heard quite correctly. *Your* patch I'll be sewing personally, and it's going to be bigger than all the others. Fat people need big patches, so they can be seen from a distance, so they won't get swallowed up in folds of fat!" And again she broke into raucous laughter, this time leading all the other workers with her in a chorus of hysterical mirth. Mother stood motionless, as if nailed to the floor, quite unable to take in what was going on around her.

"And don't forget…. don't you dare forget…" – Kitty was almost choking on her own maniacal laughter – "Don't forget to address me in future as 'most highly esteemed Madam Kitty', and now get back to your stinking pots!"

The Germans had barely shaken the dust of the road from their clothing, and already the mice were leaving their holes.

FIVE

The service in the synagogue was shorter than normal Seder night services. That Passover in Hungary, the sensation felt in many hearts was that of "Return to Egypt". And yet they all still came to the synagogue in festive attire. Clothing was another prominent symbol of the division between sacred and profane. That year, even the winter proved stubborn, refusing to give way to spring.

On the way home, after the conclusion of the abbreviated service, Father and my sister walked hand in hand, while Mother and I followed behind them.

Suddenly my sister stopped and asked earnestly: "Daddy, why are there no stars in the sky? And why have we got stars on our clothes? They never used to be there, and you always say the stars are up in the sky to watch over us from above, and light our way in the dark."

Father was unperturbed:

"Little girl, when there's a storm in the sky and the stars can't be seen, God doesn't stop loving us. He sends the stars down from above and puts them on our clothes, near the heart, so they can take even better care of us."

My sister had not been aware that God had recently changed His protection routines, and she accepted Father's explanation like Law from Sinai.

On our arrival at home, the Seder table was set up in the appropriate manner. Father donned the white shawl, Mother put on his raised chair a cushion to lean on, and I went to the door leading to the backyard and opened it halfway. The Prophet Elijah had the eccentric habit of arriving on Seder nights by the rear entrance.

The festal table was covered by a white cloth, gleaming as brightly as Father's shawl. Two candlesticks, like a proud pair of towers, reared up from the table; the two sentries stationed in them conferred in heated whispers. The traditional Seder night platter, with celery, bitter herbs, mixed fruits and nuts, shankbone and egg, held the place of honour in the middle of the table. All the Haggadahs were still closed, except my sister's illustrated Haggadah; the colourful pictures accompanying the stories drew her attention, and she was flicking through them with mounting curiosity.

Mother checked the foodstuffs for the umpteenth time and warned them not to disappoint us, when it would be their turn to be summoned to the table.

Father called upon all members of the household to raise their hands and take their places at the table. After he had blessed the wine and the occasion, the Haggadahs were opened, and the ancient legend of the Exodus from Egypt was once again under way. From time to time the story was halted, as my sister had some (unscheduled) questions to ask.

We soon arrived at the "Why is this night" section, which by tradition was allocated to me.

I had just begun chanting "Why is this night different from all other nights?" when suddenly the sound of a loud crash shook the house. The window-panes of the dining-room were smashed to smithereens by a stone thrown in from the darkness and landing on the Seder table, beside the dish of bitter herbs. By a miracle none of us was hurt, although my sister was very frightened, running to Mother to take refuge in the folds of her dress. Father maintained his composure and explained to us patiently why this night was different from all other nights.

While listening intently to my father's explanations, I remembered a schoolfriend of mine – Tommy Braun, who was reckoned a gifted lad. In one of our religion classes he challenged our teacher, Rabbi Grunzweig and asked him why God has nothing to say in these hard times. Is the reason for His silence inherent in His wisdom? Or doesn't God know how to ask questions? It's hard to cope with the idea that God is silent out of ignorance, let alone the positively sinful thought that God is silent out of malice...

Rabbi Grunzweig was stunned by the sequence of questions. He sent Tommy home, with a letter to his parents containing an urgent invitation to a meeting, to discuss the serious problem posed by their son's presence at the Jewish School.

When Father had finished reading the Haggadah, I remembered the morsel of pitta bread that hadn't been stolen. A Passover Seder without theft of the pitta isn't a proper Seder. I asked Mother to distract Father's attention, so I could perform the ritual pilfering.

After the meal we sang the "One, who knows", and waited for the arrival of the Prophet Elijah. He always used to appear on "Thirteen, who knows" (and not on "Cast your wrath upon the Gentiles," the more conventional consensus). This time, for some reason, he was long overdue and I was beginning to worry, thinking perhaps some accident had befallen him on the way. Father tried to reassure me: "Don't worry, son, he's coming, you'll see." In the meantime we started singing "This is the kid" and my sister fell asleep. Every few minutes I would get up from my seat, go to the back door and open it a little wider, to provide easier access for the Prophet Elijah. By this time my Mother was dozing too, and it wasn't long before Father closed his weary eyes and drifted into the world of dreams.

I don't remember how long I stayed at my post; I only remember that this Seder night, for the first time, the Prophet Elijah didn't visit our house.

SIX

In the summer of 1944, all trains ran in one direction. Dormant railway tracks, hundreds of kilometres in length, the rust already nibbling at them, were roused for a new lease of life. Even lines designed for movement in the opposite direction were turned around, to play their part in the renaissance of rail. The heavy wooden sleepers between the tracks, clamped to the ground with big iron pegs and shrouded in gravel, were almost smothered by the layers of moss. The concerto of train-whistles, meant to presage a new springtime for humanity, did not match the low-key appearance of the landscape, stubbornly retaining its original and primeval form.

Trains were dispatched with the regularity of volcanic eruptions. To each locomotive, at least two dozen livestock wagons were hitched, and in each wagon around a hundred head of cattle were crammed for their journey to the abattoir. I was one of them We were the first to be thrown into the mobile prison, which had three blank walls and a narrow barred window located near the top of the fourth, a necessary precaution to ensure delivery of a whole and healthy consignment. As we enjoyed the privilege of fist arrival, we naturally gravitated towards the one wall-panel boasting an aperture. My parents sank down on the floor of the wagon and I stood with my back to the perforated wall. My little sister, who had never travelled by train before, was beaming with excitement. Lack of space meant that she had to stand on my feet, her arms around me and her hands clutching my braces from behind. Loading of the wagon continued until the chorus of the buttons began. As more and more were pressed inside, the buttons of their clothing collided, producing a sound reminiscent of the clinking of glasses in a convivial toast, and it was only then that the loaders realised there wasn't so much as a hair's breadth of standing room remaining, and the heavy door was slammed shut and bolted from the outside with a massive iron bar.

Packed to the very limit, the train set out on its way, to the accompaniment of the barking of dogs – of both the two-legged and four-legged variety.

I pressed against the wall of the wagon and strained my ears to hear the clattering of the wheels. The wheels rang in my ears as if chanting a monotonous prayer: *Shema Yisroel... Shema Yisroel... Shema Yisroel...* It was as if the prayer was filtering through the narrow hatch into the interior of the wagon, and the congregation there responding in silent chorus: *Adonoi echod... Adonoi echod... Adonoi echod...*

The elderly and the infants of the community, clutching at one another for support, swayed in the cattle wagon like passengers on a ship adrift in mid-ocean, lurching between hope and despair.

My father crouched on the floor of the wagon and tried to shrink himself to the smallest possible size. His head slumped on his chest, the lids were closing over his eyes, and the expression on his face was virtually comatose. My mother, though forged of stronger materials, of steel and concrete, held within her large body a sensitive and loving heart. She too contracted her ample dimensions to the minimal, to allow her neighbours a scrap of extra living space. Kneeling beside my father, she wiped his brow with a wet handkerchief. All this time the train was spurring onward, whistling plaintively on the levels and panting uphill.

I slept on my feet. I dreamed I was going with Father to the theatre, to see a performance of "The Gypsy Baron". In the lobby of the theatre, where we arrived half an hour before the curtain was due to rise, I wandered about in a daze. The walls all around were decorated with scenes from previous productions, and portraits of famous actors. Suspended from the ceiling like bodies on a gibbet, gleaming crystal chandeliers swayed too and fro, shedding light on the busy concourse. The floor was covered by a red carpet, the kind spread at the feet of kings and aristocrats. Father saw that I was hovering in the world of fairy-tale, and he said to me in his characteristic style: "Breathe, son, take a deep breath." Then he turned to the kiosk, and bought me a refreshing drink and a slab of chocolate, which we shared between us. As we entered the auditorium, he handed me a programme. We sat in the fifth row, in the middle. Pungent perfumes assailed my nostrils, and I didn't know where they were coming from. Father told me these were the typical smells of the theatre; I was almost intoxicated by them. Members of the orchestra were taking their places in the shallow pit in front of the stage, and a medley of truncated musical sounds filled the void of the theatre as the players completed their last-minute tuning. At 5.00 precisely the lights were dimmed. There was a hush in the auditorium as the maestro – the conductor – appeared and bowed to the audience. The orchestra launched into the overture, to the accompaniment of a single large spotlight, straying across the conductor's back and touching the faces of the musicians, before finally leaping up a level and focusing on the centre of the elegant curtain separating the stage from the audience.

I sat mesmerised in my seat, since I felt myself a part of this sumptuous purple curtain, which the local theatre had ordered from my father's workshop. It was a gigantic curtain, made of a velveteen fabric which was a delight to touch and a glorious sight. My father spent hours brushing the nap on the silky surface, and whenever he touched the soft material, it was as if his whole body quivered. All the tense wrinkles that grooved his forehead eased as if of their own accord, and a faint smile flickered at the corners of his tight lips. The floor-space of our apartment was too narrow to accommodate the full size of the curtain, to let the giant enjoy his final rest before being hung in the theatre. To be approached by the most prestigious artistic institution in our city was a great compliment to my father. His pride soared sky-high when he was chosen, out of all the tailors in the big metropolis, to be the first – and the only one – to be entrusted with this monumental project of craft and design. The huge, wine-red curtain served as a kind of bridge, over which I walked into the theatrical world.

As the orchestra finished playing the overture and the curtain rose majestically, a torrent of applause swept through the audience… and my sister pulled my braces off my shoulders and howled with laughter as my trousers slid down to the floor.

The stench of excrement filled the wagon. The heat was stifling and enervating. The little air that filtered through the narrow aperture was snatched by the fitter passengers. Many had to defecate in their clothes. There were two at least with severe heart conditions, and a thirty year old woman, an asthmatic, was choking to death for lack of air. It was as if the prayers of the feeble, addressed to the One who sits on high, were coming back marked "Returned to sender".

My mother had her hands full. As it was impossible to move from place to place in the wagon, she tended the needy ones closest to her in her own little corner of Hell. With one hand she stroked my father's brow, with the other she unfastened the shirt-buttons of a groaning old man, and even while her hands were busy administering first aid, her eyes were on the look-out for others who were appealing for her help.

I wondered: from what source did she derive the strength of spirit in conditions such as these, to take on the guise of an angel? Where were the magic fountains from which she drew the droplets of love to sprinkle on mankind? And where was the tree that she was constantly visiting, to pluck the fruits of her wisdom?

I don't know how I was suddenly jerked backwards, but I remembered Grandpa Lipa, who for five years had been under the ground.

SEVEN

I used to be a passionate devotee of storks. I loved to watch them flying above the roofs of the houses. Time after time they circled about their little domain, and when they landed and settled on slates and chimneys, I would gaze at them for hours on end, feasting my eyes on their red beaks and masses of white feathers. Their slender legs could not fail to arouse envy in the heart of anyone whose own limbs were on the podgy side.

Whenever I saw a stork asleep, standing on one leg, I would try to imitate it. And even when I was under the impression that I was asleep, I always woke up when the foot suspended in the air fell to the ground with a thud, to join its partner, waiting there impatiently for its return.

I was sad to see the storks leave in the autumn, and happy to welcome them back in the spring. My love for them I inherited from my mother, who hour upon hour used to tell me of the sterling service that they perform in the survival of the human race. Whenever I saw a stork sailing through the sky in the direction of the city hospital, carrying a baby in its beak, a new arrival in the world, my heart was filled with envy. How come the storks are bringing brothers and sisters to all the other children, and leaving me out?

One morning, in the spring of 1939, I plucked up my courage and asked my mother why she wasn't asking one of the storks to bring me a sister. I could tell she was overcome by embarrassment at my astonishing question. She dismissed me with a brief and evasive answer, which wasn't like her, adding that this was a subject she would need to discuss with my father. Days and weeks passed, but I found no further opportunities to remind her of my longing for that baby, whose arrival I was awaiting so impatiently.

At the beginning of the summer, when the sun was playing fewer and fewer games of hide and seek and the streets were painted orange and gold, more and more storks were seen on their way to the hospital. One Friday, coming home from school with my shirt in tatters, I was bracing myself for a scolding or perhaps more than that – depending on whom I met first – Mum or Dad. Much to my surprise and contrary to my expectations, Mum greeted me with a smiling face and open arms. She took my satchel from me and before I could begin to recite the plausible excuse that I'd been rehearsing all the way home, she said: "It doesn't matter, dear, the important thing is that you haven't been hurt. It's only a shirt, and it's an old one anyway. I was going to throw it out."

Throughout the meal she sat beside me and never took her

loving eyes from me. Her face shone and from the dimple on her right cheek, her regular hiding-place for secrets, a little secret seemed to be about to emerge.

"Do you know, dear?" she turned to me, as I was finishing off my meal with a generous portion of apple-cake – "I've talked to Dad about the baby, and he's said he'll give it favourable consideration." I was so excited I knocked my plate off the table and it smashed on the floor.

That night I couldn't sleep. I prayed, and thanked God for thinking of me too and not just my classmates.

At this time I was sleeping on a divan in my parents' bedroom. As I was making efforts to persuade myself to sleep – all my efforts coming to nothing, such was my excitement over the imminent arrival of the baby – I heard strange sounds from my parents' bed, a mixture of fragments of speech, groans and whispers. I couldn't figure it out. Some time later, their bed seemed to lose its equilibrium, bouncing and jerking alarmingly as if occupied by a pair of drunks. I thought this was a repeat of the earthquake that had hit us last year; I would never forget the sight of pictures falling from the walls, beds dancing the tango, candelabras on the ceiling swinging and performing weird acrobatics.

I was so scared I hid under the blanket, and it seems I fell asleep soon enough.

…I was sitting on the steps of our house, facing the inner courtyard, when suddenly a flock of three storks landed at my feet. As I was still wondering at their beauty, the storks spread their wings and soared away with me into the heights. I was a bird sailing through the sky, gliding and swooping above the landscape, spread out below like a coloured carpet. We were flying in a bird-shaped formation: a stork leading and I following with a stork on either side. My senses soared above the roofs of the houses, my lungs filled with mountain air and my pair of wings beat the wind, propelling me on towards our destination, the baby-factory. After a short flight, as I was swooning with intoxication, we were once again in that aerial corridor, a child's cradle hanging from the beak of each of us. I was carrying a pretty baby girl, with little dimples on her cheeks. I imagined the look on my mother's face, seeing me arrive at the maternity ward and deposit the baby beside her. As I was hovering in a happy bubble, we hit an air-pocket, the kind I wasn't used to, and I dropped down helplessly, below the storks escorting me, and to my horror the cradle slipped from my grasp, plummeting away and disappearing from sight.

At that moment my whole world was in ruins. I cried out to the high heavens, not knowing that the walls of the sky are impenetrable.

…When I woke up, Mum was sitting by my bed trying to calm me with her soft and soothing voice. I recovered from the nightmare, much to her relief, and then I asked her about the sounds I had heard from their bed the night before. For the first time I saw my mother blush. Then she put her lips to my ear and told me in a breathless whisper that she had been talking to Dad all night, and had persuaded him to ask one of the storks to bring me a sister.

Nine months later I saw with my own eyes a long-legged stork going down the chimney of the municipal maternity ward, and putting down on my mother's bed a blonde, curly-haired baby girl.

Until the birth of my sister I had loved storks. From that day on, I admired them.

EIGHT

Four steps led to the doorway of the house where my grandparents lived – my mother's parents – which was located in a
communal yard, opposite the Nadlers' house. The advanced
age of my grandfather and grandmother didn't impair the
long-lasting friendship that developed between them and
their younger neighbours, who were teetering on the brink
of their forties.

Grandma and Grandpa were ideal neighbours. Happy are
they, whose home is their castle. In her free time Grandma
devoted herself to all kinds of needlework, sewing and em-
broidering ornaments and trinkets with coloured threads.
Grandpa on the other hand – disabled by chronic leg-pains
and needing a stick to lean on – spent whole days hunched
over albums crammed with stamps, sorting and mounting
them lovingly. He was among the leading philatelists of the
city, and his collection was renowned. He didn't know then
that his love of stamps would be inherited by two further
generations.

The Nadlers opposite – Kitty and Dury – were very fond of my mother's parents and felt strong ties of affinity towards them. Whenever they met my grandparents, they greeted them with radiant smiles. Their three children also absorbed this congenial spirit, being stamped with the seal of good upbringing – courtesy of their parents who were both teachers in the Jewish school.

I don't remember if I was drawn to girls in my infancy, or if I had a girlfriend in the kindergarten. What I do remember is, at nine years old, falling head over heels in love with Lili – middle daughter of the Nadlers. Lili was a girl of such qualities that however hard I might try to find some fault with her, I was sure to have failed utterly. She was a hybrid of brains and beauty. But the truth is, her diligence in the classroom and her academic record were about as important to me as last winter's snow, melted and streaming away into underground caverns. I was captivated by her perpetual smile, apparently embroidered on the pair of dimples which opened up delightful hollows in her face whenever the smile spread from ear to ear. Her black pupils gleamed and darted about incessantly, but what fired my imagination most of all were the two locks of hair, plaited like Sabbath hallah-loaves. I used to hold them as a wagon-driver holds the reins of his speeding horse.

…In my imagination I was speeding, swallowing vast distances from one end of the earth to infinite space, kicking out and neighing, teasing the wind with its feeble gusts, and Lili neighing and whinnying too, with all the spirit of a pedigree mare, leaving the wind far behind.

Every day I used to visit my grandfather and grandmother's house. I would arrive straight from school, strip off my satchel and sit on the third step, waiting for Lili to appear while building towers of wooden bricks on the second step.

The strangle-hold around the Jews was growing tighter from day to day. Anti-Semitic laws were issuing from the legislature in the Hungarian capital like fresh loaves from the local bakery. Jewish households were filled with anxiety, blended with hope that these laws might yet prove a temporary phenomenon and soon disappear. The market in delusions was booming.

Synagogues became a magnet for optimists. Every rumour took on wings and circled experimentally above the heads of the worshippers before smashing into the Holy Ark, splinters showering the worthies sitting by the eastern wall in the front row. Rabbis were working overtime, preaching a lot of sermons and calling upon the congregation of the faithful to put its trust in the Almighty, who would surely come to the aid of all and sundry in the time of their distress.

But while God was taking a siesta – the streets of the cities were filled with mortal dread. The crash of boots roused sleepers, and the smashing of shop-windows ripped apart the veneer of silence enfolding the cold winter nights. And the walls, they too were painted black.

And I sat on the third step at the front of Grandpa's house, building towers with toy bricks. Suddenly a scream shattered my reverie, shaking the tower I had built. When I looked up I saw Lili running, panic-stricken, trying to open the door of their house. Her mother was following close behind, moaning and wailing and tearing hanks of hair from her dishevelled head, and in the middle – four men were carrying Lili's father, bruised and beaten, blood all over his face and throat. Dury Nadler was one of the first victims of the "Cross-bow" gangs.

I was terrified by the nightmare sight and I sprang up as if stung by a scorpion and hurled myself maniacally at the door of the house, the glass panel smashing as my bare head cannoned into it. A big gash opened up on my forehead from the force of the impact. Blood was everywhere, streaming down my face in a red cataract.

"I'm dying! I'm dying!" I yelled at the top of my voice, rousing my grandfather and grandmother from their repose; they lost no time in wresting me from the clutches of the angel of death, who at that time was not yet a regular visitor to our homes. "I can't see anything!" I shouted. "I'm going to be blind for the rest of my life! I'll never see Mum and Dad again, and Grandma and Grandpa, and I won't ever see Lili again!" Suddenly I felt two tender hands caressing my face, one large and one small. Despite my proclamation of total blindness, I could make out the shapes of Lili and her mother, enfolding me with their love, having left their own precious casualty in their home, opposite. The hands of both were stained with blood and I didn't know if this was the blood of the husband and father, or mine – or maybe a mixture?

Lili said gently: "Don't cry, it's nothing serious. You'll feel much better in the morning." And her mother added in her quiet voice: "It's just a little flesh wound. It'll heal in no time, and if it leaves a scar, it means you'll always remember us." And sure enough, I was left with a scar on the forehead and every morning, when I look in the mirror, I see a pair of hands caressing my face, one large and one small…

NINE

The cheerful barking of Dobermans greeted the train on its arrival at the final station, the end of the line. When the last of the passengers had disembarked with dignity, from cattle-class, they stood us in a long line. Affable and welcoming men in uniforms, harnessed with thick leashes to the frisky Dobermans, explained to us calmly that after such a long train trip we needed to stretch our limbs, and with this in mind they had laid on a ten kilometre walk for us, the last leg of our journey to the "holiday camp" of Bergen-Belsen.

Teeming rain lashed the train passengers. Shafts of lightning and rumbles of thunder competed with the Germans for our attention. Flashes of indignation cut through the haze of sights and sounds, and we didn't know if the wrath of the Creator was being unleashed upon us or our hosts. All the roads in the vicinity had turned into tracks of clinging mud, and the route of our trek to the Bergen-Belsen holiday camp was little better than a quagmire. One of the most telling signs of the tempestuous weather was seen in the Germans' boots

– lacking their customary shine; their footwear was encased in generous layers of mire. This would be a good day for the shoe-polishers at the camp, poised even now to welcome the boots with their wet and muddy coating.

I was standing in the middle of the crowd and nobody paid any attention to my new shoes, a birthday present from my parents, but as I was already almost knee-deep in mud, they weren't particularly conspicuous anyway. When Mum told me she had omitted to bring shoe-polish, I felt the tears clogging my throat. Dad was leaning on Mum, helpless, and my sister was half-hidden among Mum's skirts. When the Germans had completed their count, the procession set out on its way, a formation like a snake beginning to crawl towards the unknown. A choral group accompanied the slowly winding snake on both sides, breaking into a stereophonic concerto of barks and snarls, while cracking horse-whips encouraged the snake to quicken its pace. As usual, it was my mother who showed leadership. Without hesitation she picked up my sister, carrying her with her right arm, and with her left supported my stumbling father, who was all the time trying to persuade her to leave him behind. As well as all this, two knapsacks swung from her overloaded shoulders. I walked in front of her, keeping within eye-shot. All the way Mum was praying to God, to give her strength, to lead us to a safe haven. Every now and then she would break off from her prayers to bolster Dad's flagging spirits, or promise my sister sweets if she'd only stop crying.

"Imre, don't go to sleep for God's sake!"… "Don't cry,

darling, don't cry,"... "Dear God, help me please,"... "Imre, you're falling asleep, wake up, we're nearly there,"... "God, give me the strength to keep them safe, give me strength and I'll be your faithful servant till the day I die, do you hear me?"... "Yes, I hear you!" – but it wasn't God who answered her, it was Dad. "I've no strength left, my dear. Leave me here... I just need to rest for a while..." The sound of cracking whips was heard close by, and my mother's face was dripping cold sweat; her lips were cracked and bitten and her legs were like twin concrete posts, striding in and out of the glutinous potholes.

The Rosenfelds' extended family walked a few paces ahead of us. Three generations in the mud. Grandpa Isaac and his wife Clara, their son Tommy, daughter Judith, and their spouses, and two grandchildren, aged ten and twelve – a devout family, in the Orthodox tradition. Isaac's face sported a neat, but dense beard, and all along the way he was reciting from the Psalms. "How great is the sin," Isaac said in a quavering voice. "It seems God has changed His mind, and is sending us back into captivity, for these are surely the days of the captivity in Egypt..." he muttered to his wife before returning to the Psalms.

Isaac Rosenfeld used to own a small grocery shop in our city, not far from our house. All the local children called him "the neighbourhood angel". He was often visited by the paupers of the district, those without a cent in their pockets, without enough even to buy a handful of flour. On Fridays he used to "sell" them hallah bread on credit, and slip slices of white cheese into their bags.

In his shop, Isaac Rosenfeld kept two account-books, to record credit transactions with his customers. On the cover of one was written "Charged to God". All credit "sales" to the local destitute were listed in this book, in the hope that God would one day reimburse him...

Even now, so far from home, he was not to be parted from the account-book; it was an inseparable part of the family baggage.

Suddenly, Isaac slipped and fell out of the line. Members of his family hurried to help him to his feet, while the incessant shouts of *Weiter! Weiter!* were heard close at hand. Attempts by his relatives to bring him back into the line came to nothing, as one of the uniformed thugs pounced on them from behind and tore him from their grasp. "Go on children, go on!" he told them. From that moment on, Isaac disappeared from our field of vision. It seems that during that thunderstorm it was important to God to settle His outstanding account with Isaac Rosenfeld. The credit and debit columns in the book were in perfect balance. Isaac Rosenfeld was left lying in the viscous mud, his glassy eyes staring up at the vault of the sky and his frozen hands keeping a firm grip on "Charged to God."

The hours passed and we were still trudging through the clinging mire without stopping for even the shortest of rests. In those hours it seemed to us that the distance between us and the Bergen-Belsen holiday camp was growing greater.

As the hands of the clock moved on, more and more gaps

appeared in the line. Many good people were left behind. My mother was beginning to panic, yet she knew there was no option but to keep on walking, without pausing for a moment. She mustered her final reserves of strength, to keep the rest of us alive. She worked tirelessly to breathe spirit into my father, and seized on an unconventional initiative as a means of keeping him awake and alert.

Mum and Dad both had fine voices. Mum in particular, who was blessed with a velvety soprano, a treat to the ears of all who heard it. Their repertoire was boundless. During the summer and early autumn, it was their regular custom to sit in the yard outside our house, especially on Sabbath eves and at festival times – and sing Sabbath and festive songs. Such nights, as the lilt of their singing reached the Heavens, all the windows and shutters in the neighbourhood were opened wide, and couple by couple, the Gentiles would stand and strain their ears to catch the melody. The residents of the nearby houses would even leave their homes, bringing stools with them and sitting in a circle round my parents.

Now, Mum sensed that he was about to fall from her grip. Her physical powers were at breaking point, and her left arm, wound around his waist and dragging him along step by step – was about to give in. As her bodily strength was exhausted, she had to muster all her mental energy, her gift for inspiration. Suddenly she put her lips to his right ear and began humming to him the prayer for the Days of Awe: "At the start of the year they shall write, and at the fast of Kippur they shall seal" – and Dad heard the tune and like a drowning man restored to life when breath is breathed into him, two little sparks appeared at the corners of his eyes.

And all this time, the skies had not yet used up all their wrath, and cataracts of water cascaded on the marchers. The Germans lashed us with whips, and angels beat the drums of thunder for us.

…The column marched on, and Mum went on singing, and the longed-for reconciliation between sky and earth was not even visible on the horizon. When the road finally came to an end Mum was still singing and she didn't stop until they had brought us safely to our temporary dream-destination – Bergen-Belsen.

TEN

The northern part of my home-town was the pride of its citizens. A dense forest of spruces and oaks encircled the northern fringes of the conurbation, and in the middle of the forest was a big lake, the haunt of black and white swans. Beside the jetty a string of rowing-boats bobbed on the water, waiting for day-trippers to take them far away from the shore, to the heart of the lake. Little islands covered with dwarf vegetation were scattered around the lake; over the years these had become the exclusive sunbathing resorts of the swans. This enchanted place was a magnet for hikers, and was known by the locals as "the big wood". I loved wandering in "the big wood" and playing scouting games. My favourite game was hide-and-seek, with numbers attached to the forehead. We would divide into two teams, and each of us would attach to his forehead a paper ribbon, on which his personal number was recorded, which we used to hide behind the trunks of the trees of the forest. Anyone whose identity was revealed by the discovery of his personal number was "burnt" and out of the game. The last player to have kept his identity secret would earn victory for his team over the opposition.

Between games I used to run to the lake, to feed the swans with bread-crumbs. At such times I used to join up with Miki, my classmate from the Jewish school. Miki was an orphan, living in the municipal orphanage. His mother died giving birth to him, and soon after her death, his father fell ill too. He contracted an incurable strain of tuberculosis, and his condition deteriorated from day to day. When he died, Miki was not yet three years old. Just as a person blind from birth is denied the joy of sight, so Miki was born without the joy of parents. His thin lips never sucked milk from his mother's nipple, and his little head never nestled in her warm embrace. He never tasted the taste of parents; the memory cells in his brain reserved for Mum and Dad remained empty and sealed spaces.

When I brought Miki to visit our home for the first time, and told my mother of his predicament, she told me to invite him on a regular basis, to be our guest at Sabbath meals. Miki's clothes were worn and tattered; every morning he would wrap himself in the same rags he had stripped off the night before and his meagre outfit did not change even on special occasions, as he had no Sabbath clothes. My father used to surprise and delight him twice a year, at Passover and New Year, dressing him in a formal suit that he'd personally tailored for him. One Sabbath, Miki arrived early from the meal, wearing his habitual expression of a doleful smile. After greeting us in his quiet voice, he was left standing in the workshop between two sewing-machines. Like a cork stuck in the neck of a bottle, neither drawn out nor pushed in, Miki stood between the machines as if rooted to the spot, as if in the clutches of a Dybbuk. We might have paid no attention to this, had it not been for the vile smell that suddenly assailed our nostrils. The stench had spread throughout the house by the time we discovered the source – a big dark stain at the seat of Miki's trousers, and lumps of excrement gliding slowly down his legs and landing in a heap on the floor. My sister burst into peals of laughter and showed him the way to the bathroom, but it was too late; he didn't need it any longer. Dad took refuge in his bedroom, and I fled to the yard, and predictably, it was Mum who took charge, overcoming her embarrassment and rushing to Miki's rescue. When she had scrubbed him thoroughly under the shower and dressed him in clean clothes, we sat down at the Sabbath table. No further reference was made to the incident; even my sister had stopped giggling. Miki's head was slumped on his chest, and the reflection of his misty eyes danced in the clear soup as it was ladled into his dish. By the end of the meal, when we began singing Sabbath songs, he had regained a little confidence and his voice rang out clearly.

I stood by the jetty and was surrounded by swans, the white ones honking away to my right and the blacks gathered to my left, as if all the residents of the lake could sense that I had arrived armed with a goodly supply of bread-crumbs. I saw Miki approaching in the distance and at once set aside a reasonable quota of crumbs for him, so that the swans wouldn't take against him but share their love between us impartially.

Miki wasn't a great talker, but I sensed something was bothering him. Without saying a word, but with a sympathetic glance, I encouraged him to rid himself of the burden.

"You know," he said, "I'll never forget what happened at your house last Sabbath. Even now the shame's making me blush."

"No need for that!" I replied. "It could happen to anyone. Something like that happened to me once at my aunt's house. And you're not just an occasional visitor to us, you're a part of our family."

"That's the way I really feel at your house," he went on, and it was obvious his emotions were overflowing. "Your mother's a wonderful woman. When she put me in the bath and washed me, I closed my eyes and for a moment it seemed to me it was my mother who was washing me. She stroked my head and said: You see, my son... yes, I think she said my son... yes, yes, I'm sure that's what she said... you see, my son, now you're lovely and clean... and she kissed me on the forehead, as if nothing had happened. No one's ever said such nice things to me before. Do you reckon your mother loves me? 'Cos I love her lots and lots."

Not far from us, beside the jetty, stood a young couple in their mid-thirties, and with them a golden-haired little girl who looked about eight years old. They stood and watched the two flocks of swans, engaged in a stubborn conflict over territorial rights in the water. For some reason it seemed to us the black swans were more agile than the white, and whenever we threw crumbs into the lake, the blacks would swipe them from under the noses of the whites. The golden-haired girl had also noticed this interesting phenomenon, and she turned to her parents and asked them, as if impelled by a sudden yearning for arcane knowledge:

"Why did God create swans in two colours, black and white?"

"To show the difference between the good and the bad," her father replied without hesitation.

"Look at the black ones, darling," the mother interposed. "Look at them, see how they're snatching food from the white swans."

"Perhaps the white swans have just eaten, and they're not hungry now," the little girl said in childish ignorance.

"No, dear, the black swans on the lake are exactly like the Jews in out beautiful country,"– the father was quick to enlighten her. "They are greedy and selfish, they are never content with what they have and they want to gobble up the whole world."

"But if God's wiser than all of us, why doesn't He tell them to stop doing that?" the little girl asked.

"Because God's sorry He ever created them," her mother answered her.

"But God has a kind heart, so won't He forgive the Jews, and have mercy on the swans too?" the girl persisted.

"No, my dear, God will never forgive the Jews, because He just doesn't like them, and they're all going to be punished for the terrible sins they've committed. God's going to chase them away until there's no sign of them left on the earth!" the girl's father declared.

When a hail of stones landed on the lake, beside the jetty, as if God had heard the innermost thoughts of the golden-haired girl's parents – the yells of the members of the "Cross-bow" gangs could be clearly heard: "Death to the black swans!" "Death to the Jews!"

When the girl heard the voices and saw the black swans fleeing in a panic to the centre of the lake, she began to run herself, suddenly darting away from her mother and father and stopping only when she found herself wedged between Miki and me. I suppose the thought never occurred to the parents, that their golden-haired daughter had found refuge in the company of two Jewish boys, whose creation God had long regretted.

ELEVEN

The brick factory in Debrecen was empty of bricks and full of Jews. The Germans had a particular affection for brick factories, in all the cities of Hungary. These were places where urban garbage could be amassed with relative ease and prepared for incineration, once the elements suitable for recycling had been sifted out.

Wave upon wave, the Jews of Debrecen and its environs were assembled on the two levels of the brick factory. Because of inflated demand for places on the upper level on the one hand, and shortage of available space on the other, late arrivals were left in the big open yard, which covered a wide area. My family found itself on the upper floor, sitting in a narrow strip of territory, each one of us clutching a meagre stock of personal possessions. Very soon our "hotel" was packed to overflowing. Group by group the families sat, huddled in circles. The conditions prevailing blurred the distinctions between the "northerners" who were considered the cream and the elite of the community, and the "southerners" who included hewers of wood and drawers of water.

Here they all sat in the same space, all appeared to be of the same height, and all had been sitting there so long, they had humps growing out of their backs. If God had a camera, and were to take snapshots of His chosen flock on the upper floor, on the ground floor and out in the yard, He would be unable to tell them apart – since all had similar faces, furrowed by the same wrinkles of anxiety, wrapped in the same veil of grief, and eyes like the eyes of fish caught in the net, endlessly seeking a route of escape.

My good mother told us all to hold hands. She believed that a circle of joined hands would generate an electrical field, a conduit whereby she could transmit her love into the hearts of us all, and fill us afresh with reserves of faith, all too liable to be depleted in this cold place, with the flag of despair flying above it. I held my father's hand to my right, and my sister's to my left, and waves of warmth began swamping our upper bodies; like the bobbing of boats moored to the jetty, we were rocked this way and that on the current of my mother's love.

The days of the Jewish ghetto in Debrecen in the spring of 1944 were numbered. There was no time to play with transition periods paced according to predetermined intervals, as required by Nazi doctrine. The arrival of Allied armies on the beaches of Normandy was imminent, and on the Russian front the tables had long since been turned and the *Wermacht* was in headlong retreat, licking its gaping wounds. The mighty Nazi war machine was on the verge of collapse.

And now it was the turn of the last Jewish community left in Europe, the Jews of Hungary – realisation of a crumbling ideology, and the swan-song of extermination. To keep to the timetable set by the Fuhrer, efforts needed to be doubled and even trebled. Fortunately for the Germans, they found a willing partner in the fulfilment of the "sacred mission", since among the Hungarian people, the devil was dancing in those days.

When I looked around me on the upper floor, I saw almost all my class-mates, huddled together with their families. Tommy Rosenberg was there too, a quiet and self-effacing lad, although his stature, as well as his perfect manners, made him conspicuous. Tommy, known as *Langer*, was the tallest in the class. I never succeeded in overtaking him, and I had to be content with second place. I remember how every week I used to run to my father, who usually had a measuring-tape hanging round his neck, and ask him to measure me. Whenever the tape revealed a centimetre's growth, I would run to school and challenge Tommy to a back-to-back height contest. Unfortunately, it always emerged that for every centimetre I had grown, Tommy had grown two. Eventually I abandoned the competition and accepted my number-two status. Tommy Rosenberg wasn't only the *Langer* of the class, he was also its most talented scholar, to say nothing of his courtly manners and his mild and unruffled temperament. His diligence and his ability to assimilate were a byword in the class. It took him no time at all to devour whole pages of text in set-books, which he would then recite by heart as if he had written the material himself, and he was nothing short of a mathematical genius; he could give the right answers before the maths teacher – the one I hated so much – had even finished asking the questions. Predictably, certain members of the class were determined to jolt Tommy – that cool-tempered guy – out of his composure, but all their efforts came to nothing.

On one occasion Willi, the hooligan of the class, gathered some of his mates together and organised them into a choir, with the express intention of goading Tommy. They chose a familiar tune and fitted suitable lyrics to it:

"Tommy Langer is a fool

Clowns about all day in school

His trousers reach up to his neck

Does he know anything? Does he heck!"

When the blessed sound of the intermission bell was heard, and the teacher had left the classroom, the choir, under Willi's direction, advanced to the podium and launched into the abusive song quoted above.

When the song was finished they remained standing on the podium in a challenging pose, waiting for Tommy's angry response. But he stood up from his seat with ostentatious composure, glanced around the classroom, undaunted by all the eyes staring at him, smiled politely at the conductor of the choir and told them in his quiet voice: "Friends, you really should learn to sing that tune properly. Don't you realise what a mess you're making of it?" At this, the whole class dissolved into howls of laughter, and Willi's fury soared sky-high.

This Willi was an incorrigible hooligan, and in fist fights and wrestling he was the undisputed champion. I once challenged him to compete with me for the role of leader of the class, in a running race over a hundred metres. Much to my surprise, Willi picked up the gauntlet that I had thrown down, and we agreed a date and a time. On the appointed day, the whole of the class assembled in the school-yard and took up positions on either side of the track. Predictably, there were two camps of supporters. At the last moment, Willi asked for a doubling of the length of the race, from one hundred to two hundred metres, working on the assumption that in my inferior physical condition I wouldn't have the stamina for the extra distance. I agreed to the proposed change without hesitation.

When we stood on the starting line, both the rival factions burst out with deafening shouts of encouragement. On the starter's cry of "Three-Ready-Go!" – I was away like a rocket, conscious that I'd got off to a cracking start. Willi must have thought so too, because he ground to a sudden halt, claiming he hadn't heard the starter. We returned to the line, and the starter asked the supporters to restrain their yells of encouragement until the runners were under way. On the second shout, which was clearly heard, I slipped and I was sure there would have to be a third attempt, but no; Willi kept on running and I had no option but to set out in pursuit, slightly delayed though I was. Our class-mates were not only shouting their heads off, they were stamping their feet too and jumping up and down. After the first hundred metres I was still trailing him by a second or two, and he was the first to touch the wall marking the halfway point. When I turned to cover the second leg of the distance, I picked up speed and felt I was riding the wave. About thirty metres from the finish, I overtook him and was sure I had it in the bag. But Willi thought otherwise. When he saw what was about to happen, he flung himself to the ground just a few metres from the line, and when I reached the tape, he was sprawled on the running track. The race was declared void, my victory was cancelled, and there were no more contests between Willi and me for leadership of the class.

Mum signalled to me to turn round. When I did this I saw, sitting not far from us, our maths teacher Mr. Schwartzkopf, with all the rest of his family. Poor fellow, he wasn't to blame for my utter hatred of the subject that he taught. I hated his subject long before I hated him. Like most of my maths teachers, he too was dry and cruel. The relationship between him and members of the class was based on mathematical principles. On entering the classroom every morning, he didn't bid his pupils "Good morning" as other teachers did; instead he would slam the door behind him, march briskly to the podium, with head held high and chin in the air, strike an imperial pose, glare at the class and after an excruciating pause, spit out his habitual theorem: "A room full of zeros – squared!"

Every teacher had a victim-pupil, someone to be picked on, and I was the "favourite" of the maths teacher, Mr. Schwartz-kopf. Almost every day I was called to the blackboard, to solve a complicated equation reserved specially for me. I had no doubt that my squirming brought him great personal satisfaction. The minutes dragged by as he kept me standing there in full view of the class. The torture session always ended with his favourite witticism:

"Eisner, if you could do somersaults and figures-of-eight in the air, you'd still be a total zero, so buzz off!"

I couldn't stand any more of these humiliations. I was determined to pay him back, whatever the consequences might be! I meant to do something that would have repercussions, that wouldn't be forgotten in a hurry, an act of reprisal appropriate for a monster of Mr. Schwartzkopf's proportions. I could hardly rely on my classmates; most of them were as timid as rabbits, and although I conferred with them, the decision had to be mine. Like all great thinkers, I knew my plan needed careful incubation if it was to be hatched successfully.

The first day back after the Passover break, the maths teacher appeared in the classroom as usual, and without the slightest deviation from his routine, gave us his customary greeting, addressing us as "Zeros – squared!" and took his seat. And it was then that the unexpected happened. His face paled, the pupils of his eyes dilated as if they were about to spring from their sockets, and his mouth opened to utter a single syllable: "No!" At once he tried to stand up from his seat, but the chair he was sitting on refused to be parted from his posterior. When he heard the hysterical laughter of the class, rolling towards him like a tidal wave, he fled, taking the chair with him. He dashed along the corridor like a runaway train to which an extra carriage had been hitched, by mistake. All the classrooms emptied as the pupils came running out, and gave him a rousing reception, cheering and applauding. When he passed the open door of the headmaster's study, he too had to put a hand to his mouth to suppress his mirth.

Mr. Schwartzkopf spent a long time wandering about with the chair stuck on behind, until he adjusted to his seated position. In the end he acquired the knack of walking while sitting, and even standing while sitting. He got used to sleeping while sitting too, because the glue that I smeared on his chair was superior stuff. I'd asked the shopkeeper for a brand of glue that would hold for at least a hundred years.

…But the glue didn't hold for even a hundred days; and here was Mr. Schwartzkopf, sitting with me and with most of his pupils, on the upper floor of the brick factory. I was minded to forgive him, and I think that I did.

The morning after our arrival in the brick factory, my mother decided we should leave the upper floor, saying we'd be better off outside in the yard. Within moments of Mum coming to this conclusion, we were already downstairs, in the yard. Later the same morning, rumours began circulating among the Jews; according to one rumour, the Germans intended to evacuate the Jews of Debrecen and its environs in three trains. Two trains would be heading for Austria, and work-camps, while the third train, carrying the leaders of the community, their families and friends, was destined for Switzerland. I don't know what invisible counsellors advised Mum to leave the upper floor, although this was where the bigwigs of the community were gathered. I regretted Mum's hasty decision, especially as most of my classmates were quartered upstairs.

The brickyard was a hive of activity, Jews running back and forth like drugged ants. All were rushing to the rumour-market, thirsty for any drops of consolation. And then, like a meteor flashing in the sky, the rumour of the trains appeared and swelled to the dimensions of a huge balloon, and anyone with a fertile imagination could see in his mind's eye the balloon ascending, laden with Jews, born under a lucky star and succeeding in making their escape to a land flowing with milk and chocolate. Some persisted in the belief that the list of the privileged was not yet full, and there were still a few places available on the train that God would be protecting. That very day there was a stampede as people began moving their possessions from the yard to the upper floor, eager to rub shoulders with the crème-de-la-crème. Besides, this floor was closer to God…

…When the train carrying the notables, those closer to God, was mistakenly diverted to Auschwitz, Eichmann was informed of the error. A flustered S.S. officer found him behind the half-open door of the toilet, buttoning his trousers.

"Herr Obersturmfuhrer," said the pale young officer, standing in the doorway and saluting his superior, "there's been a terrible mistake. A train carrying the elite of the community has been sent to Auschwitz, instead of Switzerland."

"Don't worry about it," Eichmann replied without batting an eyelid. "If it's gone to Auschwitz – it may as well stay there." He flushed the toilet.

That night, I saw my mother in a dream, with two big wings fastened to her shoulders. I knew then – she was an angel.

TWELVE

The whole class went out for a day of recreation in the "big wood". In the afternoon, when we were already exhausted by physical activities, we sat in a wide circle and reviewed the day's experiences. Elonika the teacher, the favourite of all my classmates, didn't interfere in the colourful fiesta, which reminded her of a Persian bazaar in full swing. She let us empty the balloon of adventures, inflated as it was with sensational experiences, at our leisure. Only when the hot air had been expelled, and the bulky balloon had shrunk to minuscule proportions – only then did the teacher take up the reins of the conversation and begin steering it towards more choice destinations.

Everyone, in turn, talked about his parents' house. Surprisingly enough, the classroom discipline enforced in the school found its way to the "big wood" and established itself in the heart of the circle, without requiring any encouragement from Elonika the teacher. It seemed that her authoritative figure radiated the right kind of qualities, as well as deterring any tendency to descend into chaos. Every child's story could be heard, ringing out loud and clear, without any disruptive heckling.

Peter Schindler was reckoned the most spoilt child in the class. He was the only son of very wealthy parents. He wasn't sure what his father did for a living; he only knew that he was away a lot of the time. His father didn't come home very often, and sometimes even stayed away over weekends. When that happened, his mother used to go to meet his father in the capital, to spend a few days of leisure in luxury hotels. Staff in the Schindler household usually consisted of a housekeeper and a nanny. In fact, Peter was brought up by a nanny and was educated, initially, by private tutors who used to come to his house every day. As a scholar he was head and shoulders above the rest of us. He was also learning to play the grand piano – an essential item of furniture in sophisticated circles.

At the end of the school year, Peter's father surprised his son by putting in an unexpected appearance at the prize-giving ceremony. Peter was overjoyed. His eyes lit up with flashing sparks, and glistening, rapturous tears showered his new clothes, leaving damp, happy stains on them. The ceremony was somewhat long-winded, and before the teacher had got round to announcing the outstanding pupil of our class, Peter's father rose from his seat and apologised, saying he had to hurry to an important meeting. He just had time to blow a kiss to Peter and his mother before leaving the hall. When Elonika, our teacher, called Peter to the stage to collect his outstanding pupil award and year-certificate, he broke down in tears – falling from the summit of jubilation to the depths of dudgeon. When, the next day, he showed his father the record of the high marks he had scored over the year, his father kissed him on the forehead and said he was proud of his son, and his achievement as the outstanding pupil of Class B.

Peter had spent the last year in Class C.

When the round of stories was completed, and every one of us had opened the doors of his parents' home to the rest of the class, the teacher, Elonika, addressed the pupils and said that everyone who loved his mother more, should raise his hand. A forest of hands rose in the air. "And now," – said the teacher – "hands up all those who love their fathers more." The tally of hands raised again resembled a forest, but a forest where most of the trees have been destroyed by fire, leaving a few isolated specimens behind. I myself abstained from voting, either in the first or the second round. My sharp-eyed teacher noticed this, and asked me why I hadn't raised my hand in one or the other.

"Because I love both my parents equally," I replied.

I wasn't sure that this answer was sincere.

When my father returned from a fair held in one of the provincial towns, where he seemed to have sold a lot of his merchandise, he was more genial than usual. With a broad smile that lit up both his cheeks, he called me to him and I found myself leaping into his arms. He threw me up, almost to the ceiling, and happy glances crossed in the air. Then he sat me on his knees, planted his long, thin fingers in the thickets of my curls and said that at the week-end we'd go together – just he and I – to the "Golden Bull" hotel. We'd have some fun, we'd even take a bath together.

"Super!" – I cried, and without any warning a hidden volcano of delight erupted in me, and I flooded him with the seething lava of my love. For several minutes I was prancing in the air, trying to work myself up to the very pinnacle of rapture. Then I hugged Dad with all my strength, and as our bodies entwined I felt we were both burning up at the same high temperature.

Mum looked on from the side, tears of joy streaming from her eyes.

We sat in a bath full of water in the "Golden Bull" hotel, at opposite ends of the tub. Transparent soapy bubbles bobbed in the water, riding on the saddles of the waves. Dad floated a love-boat made of paper towards me, and I sent him a raft full of longings.

Without exchanging a word we sat in the water for a long while, each of us sailing his own craft. Dad's face was nice and smooth, and his bald scalp matched the smoothness of his features, combining to create a fine, statuesque head, a pleasure to look at. He wasn't a great talker. On the contrary, my father was sparing in social conversation; the taciturn, poker-faced discipline of the card-table had taken him over, and permeated every corner of his life. I looked for ways to get him talking, and knowing he was very sensitive in the region of the waist and on the soles of the feet, I decided to tickle him. At the touch of my right hand on the sole of his left foot, he erupted in raucous laughter, trying to pull his foot away. While this was happening, our boats capsized and began sinking in the bath. We both leapt to save them from sinking, and in the process our foreheads collided, and I too burst into laughter as the water slopped over the sides.

"Enjoying this, lad?" he asked suddenly.

"I… er… yes, it's great!" I replied, choking with happiness.

"Would you like me to scrub your back?" he went on to ask.

"Oh yes, please!" I answered him – "And after that I'll scrub your back, Dad, okay?"

"Absolutely okay!" he answered with a smile.

As we scrubbed one another's backs, again the water overflowed. After a while Dad asked me to change position and sit beside him. Waves of pleasure swept over my body. Then he took my head between his hands and laid it on his wet chest. As he kneaded my golden curls, he asked me gently if I'd like to spend another weekend with him. I sensed that my voice had deserted me, and so I nodded my assent. In the end he pulled out the plug and gradually the level of the water subsided until it disappeared altogether. For long while – even when the bath was completely empty – he went on fondling my head.

This was the first bath I ever shared with Dad – and it was also the last. There were to be no more mutual caresses in the tub.

THIRTEEN

The Strausshof camp in Vienna was the biggest slave-market operated by the Germans in the Austrian sector. Any consignments diverted from their route to the extermination camps – to avoid over-taxing the ovens – arrived in jolly Vienna. At this time, the people of Austria had no shortage of reasons to be jolly. Not only had they earned the German bear-hug, they had also been given the opportunity to prove that their hatred of the Jews was far greater than that felt by the Germans themselves. Austrians had no difficulty finding corroborative evidence for this; detestation of the Jews had been a part of their heritage for centuries and their homes were virtually wall-papered with caricatures of the spawn of Satan.

The menfolk, smug and pot-bellied, gathered in bars and bierkellers, swilling liquor laced with the paradisiacal flavour of hatred. And the women, asserting their equality and not wanting to be left behind, buried their faces in perfumes reeking of Hell-fire. Even the air itself – one of the essentials of human existence – was not immune to the murderous contagion.

In this hearty atmosphere, we arrived at the slave-market of Strausshof, to be sold for a mess of pottage to an Austrian farmer.

After a thorough process of disinfection, which had the purpose of ridding us of the foul-smelling veneer exuded by our Jewish souls, we were sent to a spacious hall in the heart of the market. On the way to the hall, I saw that the market was surrounded by high wire fences, on every side. Wherever I looked, I saw nothing but tall concrete posts linked together by strips of barbed wire. Only in one direction did I see no wire fences – in the sky. Perhaps they were there too, and I just didn't notice them.

These were the torrid months of July-August, months when, in normal times, God too takes His annual vacation. I looked up at the sky, to feast my eyes on the wide expanses of the firmament, painted in bright shades of blue, like a great azure-coloured prayer-shawl.

I couldn't have known then, that the colours I was seeing were camouflage-colours.

As I reflected that this was the season when school-gates were thrown wide open and pupils flung into the arms of their long vacation, I noticed two birds' wings sprouting from my shoulders, wings without which I'd definitely have been incapable of hovering even a few metres above the ground.

As the column of marchers approached the great hall in Strausshof, a flock of birds passed overhead and suddenly, I was taken over once again by summer sensations, sensations that used to visit me at regular intervals. Instinctively I soared aloft and joined the flock, bringing up the rear. As in previous summer holidays, this time too I was powerless to resist my longings for the "big wood".

When I landed close to the swans' lake, hundreds of children and adults swarmed around me. They all stared at me in disbelief, as they had never before seen a bird come down from the sky with a yellow badge on its back.

Among the bemused onlookers surrounding me, there was one, standing in the front rank, who suddenly mustered some initiative and took two steps forward. The crowd fell silent. The man who had stepped out of the circle, in my direction, was somehow familiar to me, but despite my efforts to remember his identity, I just couldn't place him. The feet of those standing in the circle seemed to be rooted to the ground, but amid the forest of legs in the second rank, I noticed a strange movement. A little girl was making her way towards the man who stood at the front. And then I remembered. I recognised the golden-haired little girl, now trying to join her father – who was out in front of the crowd and striking a menacing pose.

"Brothers and sisters, fellow-citizens!" – the man began, ripping the silence to shreds. "Do you see the contemptible bird, with the yellow badge? It is a sign and a symbol for us. Our Father in Heaven has sent it to us now, to remind us that our lovely city has been purged of Jewish vermin. God no longer speaks through revelation on Mount Sinai, He speaks to us with signs and miracles. And He is firm in His resolve to rid the world of the contagion that has infected it. Our God is indeed worthy of our praise, and we should bow down before Him, give Him thanks for His grace and cry Alleluia!"

And the sheep in the crowd followed the lead of their shepherd and fell on their knees, looking up at the sky and crying with one voice: "Alleluia, Alleluia, Alleluia!"

"What shall we use for a sacrifice?" someone shouted.

"Yes, we need a sacrifice!" others chimed in after him.

"The bird!" yelled another. "Let's sacrifice the bird with the yellow badge!"

Mortal fear took hold of me, and then the golden-haired little girl scrambled to her feet and addressed the crowd in her shrill, piping voice:

"Please, don't hurt the yellow bird. God loves birds of all kinds and colours. Birds come to our houses every day and take children's letters up to Heaven. Please, don't hurt the yellow bird!" Her speech was followed by an awkward silence. I decided it was time to leave.

As I soared up into the sky, I saw a mass of people all rising to their feet. I saw the golden-haired little girl too; she had fallen to the ground, to be trampled beneath the cloven hooves of the sheep as they surged towards me, yelling at the tops of their voices:

"Stop the yellow bird! Catch him! Put him in a cage! Stop the yellow bird!"

Once we were inside the big hall, Mum planted us plumb in the centre. We sat on the floor and formed a tight circle around her. Hundreds of such circles were being formed in the hall, which could have swallowed us all up and been quite unaware of our presence. No one knew why we were there, in that massive space. At one end of the hall, to our right, was a raised platform like a stage, for speech-making or performances. A flight of five steps led up to the stage.

In spite of the despair that had settled among most of the Jews, as they conferred among themselves, in their family groups – there was always someone prepared to look on the bright side, to say the glass was half-full, not half-empty. In the circle closest to us, on our right, sat a family of five. Two of the boys looked to be around sixteen or seventeen. A dark-haired girl, with two plaits hanging to her shoulders, turned to her mother, a thin stream of spittle running down her chin:

"Mummy, what I'd really like now is cold chocolate and apple-strudel."

The younger of her brothers leapt to his feet, snapped his fingers, and shouted:

"Waiter! Chocolate for the young lady, and apple-strudel, if you please!"

They all roared with laughter. The girl laughed too, her plaits laughing with her and swinging from side to side. Only a sharp eye could have noticed the faint flush spreading over her pretty face.

The rising and falling wail of sirens brought us all back to the reality that we were trying to escape from. Whenever a squadron of British bombers was approaching Viennese airspace, the sirens set up a deafening racket. Silence reigned in the big hall.

The echo of the falling bombs sounded like a game of hide-and-seek. Approaching... receding... approaching again. Anti-Aircraft guns, dispersed around the city, rotated on roof-tops like giddy carousels, in their hunt for the elusive bombers of the R.A.F. All sought to shrink themselves to the size of a folding umbrella. A pair of bombers passed overhead with a menacing roar, setting the roof-tiles dancing. Three God-fearing Jews were busy opening up channels of communication with Heaven. Each of them sent an urgent telex to God; the text of the messages was virtually identical.

Suddenly, about half-a-dozen youngsters rose up from out of the silence and climbed onto the stage, in an effort to ease the tension. They began to sing, and so many joined in that the boom of the falling bombs was inaudible. There was a sudden migration of families towards the stage, and when I saw the crowd heading in the direction of the entertainment, I sprang to my feet, and urged Mum to let us shift our "domicile" to a more cheerful location.

Mum, who was capable of keeping a calm and a cool head in the toughest situations, fixed a pair of big eyes on me, while raising her right arm with extraordinary vigour, pointing her finger at the centre of the circle in which we were sitting and saying, in a loud and stern voice which wasn't like hers at all: "We're staying here. You get that? Here, right here! In the circle!"

"But even the girl with the black plaits..." I tried to protest.

"Can't you hear what I'm telling you? We're not moving a centimetre from here, even if the roof of the world falls in on us! Now sit down on your backside!"

Mum tried to say more, but I didn't hear any of it because just then we were all hurled up in the air. When we landed, we were trapped between the floor and the roof of the hall, which had come crashing down on us with apocalyptic force. For a moment, all was quiet. Then, the only sounds you could hear were the groans of the injured and the silence of the dead.

When they pulled us clear of the trap, we were witnesses to a nightmare spectacle. One of the planes had discharged a full stick of bombs above our heads, scoring a direct hit on the big hall and turning it into heaps of rubble. Of those who had been sitting to our right, towards the stage, all that remained was a dim memory. They had simply been torn to shreds. Whole families – old folk and infants included – had been wiped out of existence. In the area to our left, extending to the rear of the hall, all were alive and well. Our family was the demarcation line, dividing the spheres of activity of the ministering angels and the angels of death.

I was still in deep shock when the German sentries pushed a wheelbarrow into my hands, and ordered me to pick out from the carnage all the hands that had been waving goodbye not so long ago, all the mouths that just now had been singing morale-boosting songs on the stage, and all the hearts that hadn't survived the countdown to the start of the seven prosperous years.

They assigned me two assistants to help with the work.

When one of them laid a pair of black plaits on the barrow...
I fainted.

When I awoke, I found myself in the arms of one of the ministering angels. The eyes looking at me were my mother's eyes.

FOURTEEN

Big drops of rain competed among themselves to be the first to break on the black crust of clay, that enveloped the earth in stifling dryness. In 1939, a long summer continued for weeks on end to flex its muscles and keep diffident autumn at bay. When the vanguard of the rainfall first peered out from among the clouds, the heat-stricken populace was mightily relieved. The old men of Debrecen couldn't remember such a summer in all their long lives.

On 21 September – the date of the changing of the guard at the crossroads of the seasons – the change did not take place. It wasn't until the second day of October that the relief detachment arrived to take up its duties.

The wedding of my uncle Bela, to his sweetheart Olga, was scheduled for 21 September. The house of my paternal grand-father was a hive of activity. Bela was the fourth bridegroom of the Eisner family, and he was also the third tailor, in the parade of the family's sartorial squad. Olga, the bride, was a woman of exceptional beauty – ample charms allied to a slim frame. Her hair was a light shade of blond, the way that Nature had made it. When she put high-heeled shoes on her elegant feet, and set out for her daily promenade, her many admirers would open their windows wide, to follow the progress of her twitching rump with frank appreciation.

Olga worked in a fashionable ladies' outfitters, and was highly regarded by her Christian employers. Her outward appearance and business acumen turned her into a key figure in the shop, and of all the cards held by her employers, she was the one on which they would have gambled for the highest stakes.

Among ladies of social standing, there was no prospect of climbing the ladder of respectability, without visiting, at least four times a year, the stylish establishment of which Olga was the presiding genius.

When it was announced from the office of the Mayor, that the First Lady was about to visit the shop, they hastily changed all the flowers in the vases, including sprigs that were only one day old. The interior of the shop was a cocktail of fragrances, composed of rose-water and French perfumes.

When the lady crossed the threshold, her hosts treated her to a long speech of welcome, beginning with the sunrise and ending with the twilight, to say nothing of a series of bows in the Japanese style, plus a resounding kiss of her hand. The Mayor's wife wasn't in the habit of wasting her time for nothing. Having extricated herself from the thicket of greetings and benedictions, she made a beeline for Olga, who also bowed low in her honour.

"Olga my dear," – the First Lady began – "my engagement

book is filled to overflowing. I need you to supply me with a wardrobe for the month ahead, suitable for four special occasions, namely – two weddings, a masked ball and a formal reception in honour of the Minister of the Interior, who is due to visit our town."

"At your service, Ma'am," Olga replied politely. The special fabrics had already been removed from their hiding-places – the fabrics concealed from the eyes of mere mortals and reserved for the pompous and the privileged.

Olga spent the next three hours winding scores of kilometres of brightly coloured material around the waist of the First Lady. The selection of dresses ordered on this occasion constituted the mobile wardrobe which accompanied the Mayor's wife to all functions, where she was in the habit of changing her outfit virtually every hour.

At the lavish reception in honour of His Excellency the Minister of the Interior, in advance of which the Mayor had held innumerable dress-rehearsals, the First Lady was acting as hostess. The morning of that day, the Town Hall cleaning staff had enjoyed a windfall and been sent home early; the domestic superintendent knew that the floor of the municipal ballroom would be polished and burnished quite adequately by the long train of the dress worn by the Mayor's wife.

For more than two hours the civic couple stood, formulaic smiles etched on their faces. The hands of guests were shaken as if they were on a conveyor belt. The Mayor, in the guise of a grinning robot, inquired after the health of the guests, but since the latter were moved on every few seconds – like bottles in a soft drinks factory – their answers were given to the perplexed deputy Mayor, who was standing in the centre of the group, wondering why the guests were volunteering so much personal information about themselves.

Suave waiters in white gloves and black bow-ties resembled soldiers in an army of puppets. Silver trays laden with drinks were wafted in the air, like swings in a playground.

Every new arrival in the ballroom was announced by the majordomo and introduced to the assembled company. The room echoed to the sound of distinguished names and honorific titles.

When Olga Friedlander stood on the threshold and her name was announced, there was a sudden hush. All heads turned to the door, and all eyes were glued to Olga's statuesque figure.

Tiny elves of confusion ran back and forth in the big room. The wife of the Minister of the Interior, surrounded by a huddle of sycophants who whispered in her ear and revealed the identity of the newcomer, was the first to give voice:

"Shame and disgrace!" she cried. "Inviting a *Jew* woman to a reception in honour of the Minister of the Interior of Hungary, is like dumping excrement in a church!"

"Shame and disgrace!" the crowd echoed, voices rising to a crescendo.

"It's like taking a pig to a christening service!" piped up a fat soprano, with a face like an arse.

The flame lit by the wife of the Minister of the Interior

spread like fire in a field of thorns, and was soon licking the ears of the hostess.

All this time Olga was standing in the doorway, listening to an inner voice telling her it was time to beat a retreat. Finally, rather than waiting to be formally declared *persona non grata*, she turned on her heel and strode resolutely down the steps of the Town Hall. She heard a hearty round of applause, and the echo of the jubilation of the guests accompanied her receding shadow.

In my grandfather's courtyard it was standing room only, as a great throng of invitees crammed inside. This was the most talked about wedding of the year, and it was only natural that everyone wanted to be a part of it. If demand had been any greater, invitations would have been traded on the black market.

Olga and Bela had succeeded in turning their love for each other into something to be shared by their many friends, who wished them well with all their hearts. Even before the ceremony, the young couple were a model to be emulated.

The Kleizmers sat on an improvised stage and boosted the merriment with their playing. The canopy stood in the centre of the courtyard, surrounded by rings of joyful revellers. Bela wore a black suit, and looked every inch the bridegroom. Olga, standing beside him in her gleaming white dress, dazzled all the guests with her beauty; they stood around her as if mesmerised, staring at her with admiring eyes. The rabbi wasn't one to take unnecessary risks, and he decided to concentrate his attention on the groom. His assistant, on the other hand, less adept at controlling his impulses, was glancing surreptitiously at the bride from under the rim of his broad bonnet. He was sure he wouldn't be caught out... until he was asked by the rabbi to pour wine into the goblet. The rabbi's assistant took the bottle in his right hand, and as he slowly poured the wine into the goblet, held in the rabbi's right hand – he peered once again at the bride – and gradually the wine overflowed the rim of the goblet, and streamed down the rabbi's trousers, and trickled into his black shoes, inundating them thoroughly. It was no longer possible to restrain Olga's explosive mirth, which infected all the assembled company. When the tumult was stilled by the stentorian voice of the rabbi, only the groom was still whooping with laughter, his body wracked by such spasms, it seemed he was on the point of collapse. When the rabbi told him to put the ring on the bride's finger, the groom's hand was shaking and for some time the ring was dancing; it took considerable effort to get it threaded on the right finger.

As the text was being read, the minutes crawled by slowly. All were awaiting the breaking of the glass, which would be the sign for the revels to begin in earnest, sweeping everyone along with them. And when the great moment came, the rabbi's assistant bent down, not missing the opportunity to glance furtively at the bride yet again, this time taking in the whole vista, from top to toe – and placed the doomed glass on a narrow patch of ground, between the groom and the rabbi.

Bela raised his laughing foot, and while the crowd looked on expectantly, brought it down with considerable force on the rabbi's left foot, missing the glass by a good few centimetres. The rabbi yelled "Shema Yisroel!" – and the congregation responded with a roar of jubilation. No one heard the sound of the breaking of the glass, smashed at the groom's second attempt. All embraced around the canopy – the parents, the guests, the rabbi with his assistant and, of course, the young couple.

As Bela hugged his new wife, he put his lips to her ear and whispered softly:

"Let's get out of here, sweetheart. No one will miss us!"

The bride took the hint and smiled at him mischievously. With a carefully choreographed series of leaps, the young couple slipped away from the festive throng, and hid themselves in a side room of the house.

When the light went out in the little room, all the stars lit up in the sky, to shine on the happiness of the lovers, who were peeling off their wedding clothes and standing facing one another, wearing only their skin. Olga let her hair down, and it cascaded in long tresses to her white shoulders, and from her shoulders to her buttocks. Bela put his cheek to hers, gathering up swathes of her hair and wrapping it around their necks. His nipples clashed with her nipples and his whole body become a sensitive seismograph, preparing for the ceremony of raising the flag of love on his rearing masthead. Olga's hands groped in the thickets of his blazing body. Silently they stood face to face, their language – the language of the tongue. Olga threaded a leg between his legs, took a firm grip on him, and with a swift movement, drew him down on the bed. She lay prone, all her fibres speaking of love, and all her secret places poised to receive their welcome guest.

And he explored her like a cautious scout, seeking a safe haven. He climbed a hill, and slid down into valleys, before finally pitching his tent between her pillars.

"Do you know where we are?" – she asked.

He nodded.

"This is the Garden of Eden" – she said, and he spilled joyful tears on her breasts.

And all this time he was probing her depths, and she never stopped coming to meet him. And when they met on the summit, the moon came alight in the sky, rays of happiness gleaming in their honour.

For a long time the parents looked for the young couple, who all the time were there… but somewhere else.

When the train reached the gates of Auschwitz, Olga and her mother found themselves on the notorious ramp. Olga was holding the hand of a golden-haired little girl. Her name was Vera. A man dressed in prison clothes approached Olga furtively, and in halting Yiddish whispered to her, telling her to hand the girl over to her grandmother. The man implored her not to hesitate, to act before it was too late.

She didn't answer him, but kept a firm grip on her little daughter.

When the three of them went into the showers, before the taps were turned on, she had time to say to her mother and her daughter: "I love you."

They went up to Heaven together.

FIFTEEN

When they stuck us in the next square, like coloured pins in the map of extermination, we didn't know if God's thumb would be tilted upwards, or if through excess of weariness, it would sink in a downward direction. In the "lepers" camp of Lachsenburg – not far from Vienna – all the "parasites" were to be quartered.

When the die was cast, we were attached to the group of those evicted from Schultz's farm in the village of Pellendorf. By the standards of German morality, our family was reckoned a collection of "parasites", and the number of "parasites" in our midst was beginning to exceed the number of productive individuals; when "producers" were weighed against "consumers", the latter definitely had the edge. My mother's eagerness to volunteer for extra shifts in the field, in addition to my own meagre contribution to Schultz's war effort, wasn't enough to expunge the stain of "parasitism" that had clung to us, and expulsion from Pellendorf was therefore inevitable.

And so we were on the road again, with our staves and knapsacks.

The little family convoy, which now included my grandpa on my father's side, wound its way through a dark, and dense, endless forest, without so much as the narrowest of apertures, through which the pale light of a lantern could be threaded.

On the way we lost Dad.

It seems that at one of the twists in that pitch-black and merciless labyrinth, Dad was seized by an angel, and there was no knowing if he was numbered among the ministering angels, or was one of a different kind.

The cup of my mother's grief was running over. She didn't blame anyone, except herself. All the arrows that she shot, she shot at herself. Suddenly, I was aware of Dad's absence. I was used to the sound of his long silences, which had ended abruptly. I felt something had been taken from me that was part of my being, as if I had stopped being whole.

Although Dad was never one to cosset me to any excessive degree – leading the busy life that he did – not a day passed in my short life without me setting out for my daily hunting expedition, searching him out, catching his eye for a split-second, which would stay with me until I lay in bed at night, until Mum handed me over to the sentry at the gate of dreams. Next day, it would all start again. From early morning onward, I dogged his footsteps.

Sometimes I'd lie in wait for him on the stairs of our house, to be the first to greet him on his homecoming; sometimes I used to creep – like a stowaway on a ship – among the rolls of soft fabric that were strewn about the factory, and get as far as the end of the massive table, which was his regular post, watching his strong hands as they subdued the layers of material, with the aid of his faithful tailor's scissors.

Mrs. Weiss, who was approaching the final third of her life, and had been a regular visitor to our house, tried to console my mother, with words of comfort and encouragement. She said it was forbidden to give up hope, especially seeing that the responsibility for preserving the rest of the family rested on Mum's shoulders. She also said she had a feeling that Dad would be found, and come back to us soon. She promised that in this spirit she would transmit her prayers to the next world.

Two days later envoys came to impart to us the bitter news of Dad's death. Grandpa told us we should sit for the statutory seven days. We were already sitting; we were sitting all the time – but this time it was different. Mum sat on the floor, with my sister and me at her side, and held us tightly; it was the same posture as before, but for a different purpose. My sister, who was used to Mum's warm cuddles and loving smiles, was alarmed to see her face stricken with grief and she wondered if she herself was to blame: had she done something she shouldn't?

Amid the silence that enwrapped us, the whinnying of horses was heard. We were "sitting" not far from the stables, since Lachsenburg had once been a prosperous estate, adapted to the needs of the twentieth century. Carriages used to come and go at the gates of the citadel, harnessed to fine thoroughbred horses.

I remember one Sunday, Dad gave up his card-game at the "Golden Bull" and took me on a two hour excursion in a black, highly-polished carriage. The driver was also in his Sunday best, with a broad-brimmed hat on his head, and shod in gleaming boots, and the fine horses, in their imposing harness, were the colour of night. Were it not for the reins in his hands, the driver could have been taken for an aristocrat on the way to his wedding; he sat proud and erect in his seat, controlling the horses in an imperious manner. Dad and I sat behind him in the open carriage, unable to cope with the swirls of pleasure flooding our faces. Out of all the trips available – short and medium – Dad chose the longest. Our bodies soon grew accustomed to the rhythm of the carriage's motion, and we strained our ears to hear the beat of the horses' hooves. Their tails swung from side to side with iron discipline, as if obeying the instructions of the driver, who sat on his seat like the conductor of an orchestra.

The first stop was Dari Square, where every Sunday crowds used to gather to listen to the music of the firemen's brass ensemble, which regaled the public with a series of brisk marches, fit to make any heart beat at a faster rate. My eye was caught by the refreshing sight of a group of little girls, dancing to the tunes of the band. Dad noticed my pre-occupation, and correctly interpreted my wistful glances.

In typically economical style, he asked me: "Would you like to have a little sister, son?"

"Yes please," I answered him just as briefly.

"So be it, then," he said without further elaboration, and

ordered the driver to carry on to the next destination.

We travelled the full length of the main street, to the city's main railway station at its western end. Here too there was a big square, full of vibrant life. The trams arriving at the station one after another disgorged hordes of passengers, all in a desperate hurry to catch their trains – and avoid a long wait until the next.

I had heard so much about the great and fine city of Budapest, Hungary's capital, that I was all fired up with curiosity, and was eager to get to know the place.

Dad seemed to be reading my thoughts:

"Like to come with me to Budapest some time?" he asked laconically.

"Oh yes!" – it came out as a barely repressed howl.

"I'll take you there soon." The subject was closed.

Then we travelled along the street where the theatre was situated, and paused for a while outside it. The matinee performance was about to start and the building seemed to be under siege, thronged by eager theatre-goers – parents and children all in their smartest attire, intent on enjoying one of the popular operettas.

"Starting next Sunday," – my father's voice broke through the armour of his silence – "you could be among those happy people, son."

"I'm happy now," I answered him briefly, content to take an advance on the promised happiness.

When we parted from the driver and his horses, for a long time I was looking up at the black carriage; strangely, the more it receded from us, the more it swelled to the dimensions of a heavenly body, shedding a dark lustre.

Three days had passed since we sat down for the seven days of mourning for my father, and the fourth was knocking on the gates of our lamentation. The coterie of comforters continued its routine unchanged. The "parasites" of Lachsenburg had all the time in the world at their disposal, and what better pastime was available to them than consoling the mourners? For this reason they came to us every day to share in our sorrow.

Mum was in a state of sustained shock, and for four days she had been uncharacteristically silent. Grandpa, a taciturn man by nature, was busy all day reciting the Psalms. My mother's silence had a devastating effect on my sister, who sat there in a state of gloom and despondency, not knowing the reason for her despondency. I wanted to talk, and especially I wanted to ask questions about Dad, but I soon realised the time wasn't ripe for this.

The evening of our fifth day of mourning, there was a sudden commotion at the entrance to the hall, where we were sitting. Almost all sprang to their feet and ran in the direction of the door, where a tight knot of humanity had been formed, uttering cries of jubilation. We remained sitting in our places. Gradually the knot dispersed, moving aside and receding like the waters of the Red Sea, when God revealed dry land between them.

And on the path thus created, my dead father was walking... very much alive. When he reached the circle of mourners, a tidal wave of joy swept into the hearts of all and little bells tinkled in our heads, proclaiming to the world the return of my father, alive. For a long time people were exchanging loving pinches, to be sure that this was real and not just a dream.

When Dad told of his experiences in the hospital in Vienna, where he had been taken by a man who had not sold his soul to the devil, a germ of hope began to steal into our hearts.

And when Rabbi Feldmann, one of God's regular houseguests, informed us that, bearing the circumstances in mind, my father had been sentenced to a long life, we believed every word he said.

SIXTEEN

Autumn is a season of transition. In this season there are clouds that waft above the rooftops, others that remain suspended, and others still that are detached from the umbilical cord binding them to the Lord of the firmament, and they descend to the sources of water, to be absorbed into them.

The universe is ruled by four seasons. Of these two are major – summer and winter – while the others serve them and mediate between them. Such is the autumn, constituting the tongue of the balance between the great ones, servant of two masters. The autumn has to steer a course, such that its territorial integrity will remain intact even when the summer is sending its heat to bite chunks out of it, and when the winter comes early and unleashes sudden winds and hailstones, to subdue it ahead of time.

But the autumn has one special feature all of its own, its crowning glory – the month of Tishri. In the month of Tishri – since the creation of the world – the Lord God of Hosts has been lowering ladders down to the face of the earth.

In the closing months of 1943, the summer ruled unchallenged. In the orthodox synagogue in our town they were polishing the habitation of the Lord, in readiness for the Days of Awe, in the month of Tishri. Leaders of the congregation did not foresee in those days, that the flocks of birds, accustomed to migrate through the skies of Europe, would not be rising aloft, because the skies were red – tongues of fire licking the fringes of the firmament – and hundreds of thousands of birds remained grounded in the frozen fields of the continent.

God, as is His custom in the month of Tishri, sent ladders down to the birds as well, but they preferred to spend the winter under a blanket of snow, rather than be roasted in the burning sky.

In our house, preparations for the festivals were in full swing. My mother was moving pieces of furniture from their places, to do battle with the deposits of dust and dirt that had found themselves a comfortable billet in the dingy corners of the room, where the bulky furniture afforded them a degree of protection. Mum used to climb a small ladder in her pursuit of the elegant webs of spiders. Were it not for the calendar, showing it was the beginning of Tishri, it would be easy to be missed into thinking this was the month of Nisan, with my mother clearing the house of impurities with the devotion of an upright Jewish wife.

When times were normal, month by month I used to pluck a page from the calendar. In the run-up to festivals, it seems I was eager to speed up the process, being infused at such times with currents of burgeoning emotion, blended with natural curiosity.

The season of festivals is also the season of presents, and because my father was such an artist in the tailoring craft, he used to surprise us with festive garb, the most attractive and stylish costumes imaginable. The special fabrics, intended for special events, were kept in a secret place in the attic. He used to climb a ladder to withdraw the treasure from its hidden niche.

When the materials had been turned into festival attire, again a ladder was needed, so that we could climb – my sister and I – onto our father's upright neck, and from there move on smoothly to the bare expanse at the top of his head, until the strength of one of use gave out and we would sink into his lap to rest a while, and fall asleep there, sated with mischief.

Not far from our house, through the chinks in the sealed windows of the ground-floor apartment of a modest tenement, situated at the corner of two quiet streets, emerged musical sounds of fluctuating volume. A wayfarer, finding himself by chance in the neighbourhood, would slow his pace and strain his ear to hear, to take these melodic sounds with him as a permanent souvenir.

Three aged cantors lived in that house. Its walls were a repository of sounds, resounding from generation to generation and passed on as a legacy from father to son and onward to his seed and the seed of his seed, generation after generation.

The cantor of the orthodox synagogue – Samuel Braun – a scion of red-bearded cantors, was tall of stature and broad of build, in a manner befitting cantors of lyrical tenor expression.

In his mighty voice he used to leap from octave to octave and spring from one rung to another on the unconventional tonal scale.

A whole congregation – purifying itself for the eve of the New Year and waiting for its envoy to speak. On the Day of Judgment he will set forth his humble entreaties before the Creator of the world and ask that every man and woman of the congregation be registered in the Book of Life, at least for one more year, until this plea can be made afresh.

The eve of the festival, the synagogue was aglow with dignified light. Most of the benches, tending to be orphaned between one holiday and the next, once again creaked contentedly beneath the weight of their sedentary occupants. Fathers, sons and grandsons, dressed in their finest attire, gathered together to lay their supplications before the Creator, in his temple,

The white robes of the worshippers revealed a fissure and concealed two fissures in their mournful souls. Wrapped up in themselves and huddled under their talliths, furrowed with wrinkles and heavy-hearted, they sat side by side, aristocrats and beggars, youngsters and those old enough to understand, representatives of an affluent community in a large provincial metropolis. In the airy void of the synagogue hovered the reverence of the Days of Awe. All were busily engaged in weighing: the balance between sins on the one side, and the tally of good deeds on the other. The last days – before the veil of the festival was drawn aside – stood as a symbol of the despairing attempts of every man and every woman of the

Jewish persuasion to tilt the scales in a favourable direction. And yet, deep foreboding gnawed at the hearts of the congregation of worshippers, every one of whom was anxious to know what be written, and how the parchment of his fate would be sealed for the coming year.

The women's galleries almost collapsed under the weight of the fear of the Jewish mother. Swathes of clinging perfume, the glitter of gold ornaments, fashionable fabrics tailored in strict accordance with the canons of haute couture, regal crowns of tumbling curls – none of these were of any avail, when faced with the raging whirlpools of helplessness and the knowledge that there was no way out.

And suddenly, like a spark in the darkness, like a scrap of dry land in the heart of the ocean, in the midst of the synagogue, the solid figure of a man-mountain rose to his feet. With stately mien he approached the Ark, and all at once the buzzing of the hives was stilled and silence fell in the hall. All eyes were fixed on the heavenly crown he wore on his head, and all ears were attentive to his utterances, and all hearts beat as one. And already the voice of the cantor was rising higher and the cry seemed to break forth: "For the sin that we have sinned before thee" and this was followed by the invocation "How many shall pass away and how many shall be born" – and it touched the despair creeping through the tissues, as if all was written and all was sealed, and all balances were tilted on the positive side, and all that remained was doubt:

Who by fire and who by water? Who shall live and who shall die? Who by the sword and who by the noose?

And suddenly, like a peal of bells on a new morning, from the gates of Heaven a deluge of ladders came raining down, ladders with their feet planted in the ground and their heads in the clouds, and all the people rejoicing and gladly climbing and going up… in smoke.

And at the end of the year, in the month of Tishri, in the Days of Awe a new phrase was incorporated in the ancient prayer: *Who by fire and who by water? Who by* the *sword and who…by the ladder?*

And God saw that it was good!

SEVENTEEN

All that my eyes could see were tall towers, rearing up from the horizon-line to dominate the landscape. Their multiple turrets were manned by sentries who had a taste for orchestral music… especially the kind played on machine-guns. Dense wire fences shielded us from the lashing of the wind, which in the winter of forty-four was more ferocious than ever.

"Welcome to Bergen-Belsen!" – the cry of our hosts rang in our ears from all the fences and all the towers. Through the pall of silence that hung over the camp, we could just make out the faint murmur of distant human voices. Ziggy Hirsch, the German teacher in our school, swore that he heard a choir, chanting lyrics of Heinrich Heine. Later it emerged that at the southern end of the camp – the apparent source of the voices – there was a large compound used for the training of dogs.

When the last of the marchers had dragged himself into the camp, all strength exhausted, the gates were sealed with materials designed to kill off any aspirations towards freedom. They lined us up on the parade-ground, which was surrounded by members of the choir, those whom the German teacher had previously heard singing. We were ordered to remove from our faces all expressions of grief, and replace them with declarations of joy. We then had to straighten our hunched backs, stick out our chests and stand proud and erect. Rain was still cascading down from the sky, like the Falls of Niagara, and the deluge cleansed our bodies, ensuring that we would be worthy to play our part in the welcome parade.

After a while, the rains ceased, and a teasing sun peered out from between the towers. Now that we had been infused with happiness and optimism, they introduced us to a dog – holder of the highest rank in the canine hierarchy of the camp. General Hund, they called him. General Hund put us at our ease and told us that we had arrived at a place of comfort and relaxation. It was the corridor leading to Paradise, no less. He added, by way of further reassurance, that anyone trying to escape, or caught stealing food, would have his sojourn in the corridor curtailed, and be dispatched directly to Paradise.

When General Hund had finished barking, he asked if we had any questions.

No one dared take the initiative and respond to the invitation. But the General was insistent, and after a while a faltering hand began to climb into the air; it belonged to a skinny, stooping man in his prime, someone who, if hired as a scarecrow, would – one suspected – have the utmost difficulty deterring any birds at all.

"I would like to know, Herr General," he began cautiously – "what will our daily routine be in the camp? Will the apartments we are given have bathrooms *en suite*?" The diminutive questioner had a perfectly respectable hump on his shoulders, and judged purely on outward appearance, could have been a carbon copy of the great Quasimodo himself.

The astonished General had some difficulty locating the source of the voice, which was already boosting the adrenalin levels in his blood. Those surrounding him were in something of a dilemma; their impulse was to break into howls of unfettered mirth, but they didn't dare stimulate their hilarity-glands without some signal from their master, if only a flicker of mouth or of eye.

Meanwhile, the questioner was feeling more self-assured, as breezes of energy filled his sails, impelling him towards the front rank of his squad.

"I would also like to know, Herr General," – he said with ever mounting confidence – "where is the nearest post office, and do you have a cinema here?"

General Hund looked to the right, looked to the left, and the signal was given. The giant balloon, suspended in the air and fully inflated with malicious and demonic laughter, burst all at once at the prick of the General's pin. Restraints were swept away. Cataracts of mirth flew from the maws of the Germans, threatening to flood the entire camp. They howled, and yelled, and stamped their feet – a mishmash of hysterical sounds swirling in the air. Their faces were contorted, their veins popping, and paunches dancing the Charleston, going up and down like a high-speed lift in a skyscraper. Even the four-legged dogs joined in the chorus, laughing in tandem with their two-legged counterparts.

The unfortunate questioner was assailed by fear and regret. He denounced his own rashness and folly. He was beginning to realise that out of that huge crowd packed into the parade-ground, the crowd towards which the General's lure had been cast, he – and only he – had swallowed it. He wished the earth would open at his feet and gobble him up there and then; this was his fervent prayer to God.

The name of the small, fate-blighted individual was Kleinmann, Pitzi Kleinmann. He lived on the outskirts of the city of Debrecen. In the corner of one of the courtyards stood an old building, which judged by outward appearances could have been an abandoned warehouse. There he resided, lived his life, rolling his days from page to page of the calendar. The man was childless, in his mid-forties. His "house", neglected on the outside, was humble on the inside as well, but always tidy and clean. No one ever identified himself as a close relative of Pitzi Kleinmann.

His livelihood depended on his regular visits to communal institutions and to the homes of kind-hearted Jews. He used to walk the streets and was often harassed by children who used to hurl insults at him, most if not all referring to his multiple disabilities.

He derived an additional, meagre source of income from – foretelling the future; he made every effort to gain recognition as a clairvoyant. I myself occasionally set aside a few coins from my weekly pocket-money, in case I needed his services. When my mother was in the sixth month of her pregnancy – and I hadn't noticed this, as I was still waiting for the stork to come visiting – Pitzi Kleinmann prophesied to me that in the near future I would have a brother or a sister. He went on to say that I didn't need to pay for the tidings in advance; I could defer payment until after the event. A gesture such as this on Fitzi's part showed a great deal of self-confidence, and steadfast faith in his prophetic gifts.

Ziggy Waldmann was a boy of nine years old, and more than anything else he loved playing with his collection of dolls. His mother was embarrassed by this, and she sought the help of Pitzi Kleinmann, wanting to know when her son would give up playing with dolls. At least once a week she would visit Fitzi's "house", for a consultation. He assured her that the day of Ziggy's weaning away from childish games was approaching. Secretly, Fitzi would have liked to postpone this day into the furthest reaches of the future. Deep down he knew that if and when the miracle happened, Eva Waldmann – Ziggy's mother – would cease her weekly visits. Eva Waldmann was a woman in her early thirties, whose rare and stunning beauty preceded her, like smoke before fire.

Although she was unaware of it, she was the essence of Pitzi Kleinmann's life, his elixir of youth. The routine of his day was planned and arranged according to her regular visits. Eva never imagined that Fitzi's days of anticipation were encrusted with the green of hope, and his nights painted with the blue of dreams.

No one knew where the keys of his heart were hidden. He strove jealously to keep his inner world safe from public exposure, lest the slightest hint of calumny be attached to him.

One thing he did allow himself – licence to dream. To dream all night, without awakening, dream that the nights would never end. In his dream, he used to stand and watch, and see the lovely Eva in a transparent chemise, writhing sensuously in her bed. He doesn't approach her, doesn't touch her, except with his eyes. Only with his eyes will he knead her snow-white breasts and slake his thirst, gorging on her nipple; only with his eyes will he lick the sweetness of her secret place, tasting the juice of her dripping honeycomb, and only in his eyes will her round buttocks heave, with the ardour of a bride on her wedding-night.

When the General had wiped his laughing eyes, awash in a sea of joyful tears, they were opened to seek out the hilarious questioner, who in the meantime had managed to retreat to a position of some strategic depth, far from the probing eyes of General Hund.

Dragged from his hiding-place by a pair of thugs, he was hoisted high in the air and piloted to the "landing-strip" at the General's feet, where he was parachuted to the ground. Having descended from the heights, he found himself licking the mud-spattered boots of General Hund.

All the dogs in the vicinity wagged their tails in pleasurable anticipation.

The column advanced – trampling, stamping and dancing

on the back of the cripple. Only when his hump was flattened, were the festivities suspended. In jovial mood, sated with the wine of sadism, the General ordered that the ironed-out hunchback be taken to his new quarters, with the *en suite* bathroom. Two gallant men lifted him high in the air, and dumped him in the nearest cess-pit…

At that very moment, the treacherous sun slipped away, and disappeared behind the tall towers.

EIGHTEEN

True to her promise, Mum took me to the little railway-station in Debrecen, and sat me down in the reserved carriage of a passenger train, which among the intermediate points on the way to its distant destination, used to stop at the station of the village where my Aunt Elizabeth lived, my father's sister.

Ever since I was a baby – and perhaps even before then – Mum had been telling me almost every evening, on the verge of sleep, that one day I would be a little man, and I would travel on a grown-ups' train. I'll sit beside the window, and an uncle in a blue uniform will come and check my ticket and ask me where I'm heading for. And I shall answer him, my eyes sparkling: "I'm going on my first summer holiday, uncle." He'll ask if I'm not afraid to be travelling alone, and I'll shake my head and say:

"Not at all! And you know what, uncle? After the long holiday I'll be starting in Class A." And the uncle in the blue uniform will smile, punch a hole in my ticket and before continuing on his way he'll stroke my head and say: "My boy, did you know that you're already a little man?"

Mum stood on the platform and waved goodbye. Through the window-pane it looked as if her eyes were glistening, flooded with moisture. When the wheels of the train began to move, I thought for a moment that the platform was travelling backwards and Mum was receding from me, in the opposite direction. Then I realised from the jolting of the carriage that I was the one moving, and my big Mum was shrinking to the size of a stick, then a ball, then a button, then a pinhead, and in the end, nothing at all. She disappeared as if she had never been. I pressed my face against the window and through the glass I saw oak-trees dancing before me, bowing their heads to me as I passed. The carpets of red tiles seemed to be leaping from roof to roof, hurrying to cover the bald heads of the houses.

Waves of joy swept over me, on my maiden voyage by train. I wasn't afraid at all. Although I was alone, I felt I had travelling companions: the train, me, and my dream. The three of us were setting out on a journey together, and we were going to have a good time.

The train whistled and whinnied merrily, knowing that its winding track lay across level ground: there wasn't so much as the faintest shadow of a hillock on the horizon.

At the same time, my dream was careering out of control, confronted by its realisation. Throughout the journey my dream was urging me into impetuous motion, a bugler sounding the charge.

And I – running hither and thither, moonstruck, between

dream and reality.

In the end I dozed. I dreamt I was in a field, without beginning and without end. I was walking in unbounded spaces, a shepherd's crook in my hand and a flock of bleating sheep trailing behind me. Little round bells were hung around the necks of the bellwethers marching at the head of the demonstration, which had the slogan: "Sheep will not go like lambs to the slaughter." Every time the bells rang, the flock answered them with a bleat of approval.

When the sun climbed to the highest turret of the sky, I lay down in the field and slept. The echo of the neighing of horses – like a distant roll of drums – crept into my ears. Three horses and one rider – a tiny figure – galloping towards me. As they raced on, the little rider leapt from horse to horse, as their manes mingled in the wind. The horses were branded with the seal of a faraway place, and you could tell by looking at them, their running had lasted too long. Two of them ran bare-headed, and seemed to be mourning the loss of their dear ones, while in an effort to compensate for their bereavement, the remaining rider jumped from horse to horse at regular intervals. When the group came into the focus of my vision, I realised that the little rider was me. I rode on the back of one of the doleful horses was "Lightning". It was obvious the horse wasn't satisfied with me, and was in no mood to accept me in place of his regular rider, who had been left behind. He made every effort to unseat me. He bucked and whinnied, galloped and jumped like a steeplechaser, and finally reared on his hind-legs, flailing his forelegs at the heavens and roaring out his imprecations, appealing for the aid of the Creator in getting me off his back.

Heartened by the advice he received, he galloped with renewed energy, approaching a branchy oak-tree which dominated the flat landscape. He rounded it once, then twice, and nothing happened. It wasn't until the third pass that he succeeded in snagging me on a branch, slipping away from under me with a snort of gratitude to the Creator. I tried with all my strength to hang on to the branch, swinging my legs and trying to wrap myself round it, but without success. I fell to the ground, bruising myself all over.

"Storm", my faithful mare, stood beside me, weeping and caressing my bruised leg with her splendid mane.

When I awoke, the hairy hand of a bespectacled, red-faced and bearded uncle was caressing my left leg. I sat up with a jolt. The bespectacled uncle smiled at me and told me not to be afraid; he was stroking me because he liked children. I remembered that on the way to the station, Mum had warned me to avoid smiling uncles with wandering hands. I wasn't sure exactly what she meant, but I was too shy to ask. The bespectacled uncle began nudging up closer to me, as if someone was pushing him, and put his hand on my trouser-buttons. I didn't know what to do. My mother's words of warning were running around in my head and at the same time, the bearded uncle's hairy hand was massaging my crutch. I couldn't understand why he was doing this. Why *there* of all places? If he really liked children, why wasn't he stroking my head, or my face?

Suddenly I felt I needed the lavatory. I was afraid I was going to lose control of my bladder and wet his hand, and then the smiling uncle would be cross with me. I tried as hard as I could to hold back. I thought of turning for help to the other passengers in the carriage, but I saw they were all asleep. The bespectacled uncle saw this too, and that was when he unbuttoned my trousers and slipped his hand inside my underpants. I realised no one was going to help me, so I changed my mind and stopped trying to restrain my bladder.

As the bespectacled uncle was bending over my open trousers, a mighty jet suddenly gushed from my willy, that he was clutching in his hand, swamping his face and washing his glasses. A sizable quantity of the torrent even penetrated his gaping mouth, and he didn't know whether he was supposed to swallow it or spit it out. As if bitten by a scorpion he shied away and leapt to his feet. And then the door of the carriage opened and the uncle in the blue uniform asked if everything was okay. "Everything's just fine," the other uncle replied, the one with urine running down his face, and he slipped away into the corridor. The uncle in the blue uniform waved at me in a friendly way and I waved back, with half a smile. Luckily, he didn't notice the big puddle on the floor of the carriage.

None of the passengers woke up. They all smiled in their sleep as they inhaled the aroma of fresh piss.

The train stopped at a god-forsaken station in a remote village, its location on the map subject to doubt. An old wooden board – riddled with cracks providing overnight accommodation for insects – bore the name of the place, which was impossible to decipher on account of the worms of time which had nibbled at it. The station-master, who stood on the rickety platform and saluted the train as it arrived, had been appointed to his lofty status by virtue of his proficiency at saluting, scoring high marks in the tests, where this was the sole qualification required of candidates. Beside the station-master's cottage stood a solitary rose-bush, and when not waiting for the train, which used to call at the place once on alternate days, the station-master's job was to tend the pair of roses growing on this bush and make sure they didn't expire prematurely.

I was the only passenger to alight at the station, and I ran straight into the arms of my Aunt Elizabeth, who was waiting on the platform with her two children, Babu and Diori. As we hugged, I sensed my aunt flinching, and she asked me at once why my mother had sprayed with this peculiar brand of eau-de-cologne. I explained that the smell I was giving off was actually the smell of cattle-urine, which one of the rustics had been carrying with her in a big milk churn, to be used for treating open wounds. During the journey the lid of the churn had fallen off and the contents had splashed all over me. I had the impression that the explanation I gave was accepted by my hosts.

We travelled from the station to the farm in a cart, and all the way my aunt was busy repelling the swarms of flies that were clinging to my wet trousers in sheer ecstasy.

My aunt's husband, Sandor, was a classic example of the horny-handed farmer. His life was ruled by the calendar of the seasons, and from sunrise to sunset he toiled to bring forth bread from the ground. Aunt Elizabeth, on the other hand, loved animals, and all day she tended them with unstinting devotion. When the cackle of chickens faded away, the lowing of cattle was heard close at hand. And in addition to this she cooked and cleaned, laundered and ironed, and still found the time to cherish her offspring.

Babu was three years older than me. A girl with blond, close-cropped hair, she was tied to her mother's apron, and her whole world was confined within the perimeter of the farm. Unlike her, Diori at twelve was old for his age, and on the verge of premature adolescence. If the farm had pillars, he was undoubtedly one of them, and the handling of the horses was entrusted exclusively to his skilful hands. In the family he was known as the "king of the stable".

When the cart arrived in the farmyard and Diori unhitched the horse and started dismantling the harness, I wanted to stay with him and see the stable, but my aunt escorted me ceremoniously to the farmhouse, at the back of the yard.

"The first thing we have to do," she announced solemnly – "is get rid of the smells that have stuck to you, and for that we need to boil water, put you in a tub and scrub your skin until the pong has gone for good."

I sat in a tub full of almost boiling water. Aunt Elizabeth, together with an assistant, scrubbed and scoured, kneaded and scraped my skin, until there was barely enough of it left to cover up my flesh. I didn't know which was worse, the scalding water or the torture inflicted on my body. Having no choice in the matter, I bore it in silence, the silence of a dying fish.

When the disinfecting process was over, and the smell of urine had been dispelled from my body, my patience snapped. I paid no attention to anyone, grabbed some light clothing and ran barefoot into the open fields that were calling to me from afar. A few metres from the farm, I came across a stick, and there and then I turned it into a speeding horse.

It was midday and the fields shimmered in the heat, in colours of orange and gold, and I was in a whirl, spurring and egging on my mare to quicken the pace, to catch up with the horizon, that was playing hide-and-seek with me, and teasing me mercilessly. However close I came to touching it, it always slipped away from me like a fish escaping the net. In my pursuit of the elusive horizon, I stumbled into a patch of sunflowers. Every one of them was the size of the sun, and there were even some that looked bigger. The big sunflowers, with their circular blossoms, used to make it a regular habit to compete with the sun, baring teeth at it, sticking out tongues at it. And the wily old sun smiled complacently and blasted the sunflowers with killer-rays, to burn out their tongues.

Suddenly I felt sharp pains in the soles of my feet, as if I was walking on a floor strewn with nails, all of them piercing my flesh. Blood streamed from my feet and when I looked around I realised I had strayed into the very heart of a field of stubble. It was like blundering about in a minefield, thousands of short corn-stalks threatening to drown my first summer holiday in my blood. I stood there as if paralysed, unable to take a step in any direction, alone and hemmed in by flesh-piercing stubble. The hours passed, and I was like an alien plant, stranded in hostile territory.

When the farm was in darkness, and members of the household gathered together, their day's work done – only then did they notice my absence. Everyone had assumed someone else knew of my whereabouts, and when I failed to appear, the farmhands were drafted in to make a wide-ranging search. Armed with paraffin lanterns they set out in pairs to scour the terrain. There was only one topic of conversation among them: who would get to me first – they or the jackals? For some months it had been known that a pack of jackals was active in the area, and fears for my safety were all too justified.

When the spear-head group reached me I was on the verge of fainting, and I don't remember if I had the strength to share in their jubilation. A few minutes later I was back in the farmhouse. Aunt Elizabeth, a wealth of experience behind her, didn't lose her composure when she saw my bruised and bleeding feet.

After yet more cleansing and disinfecting, my feet were wrapped in a double layer of bandages and I was put into bed. Members of the family stood around my bed and said nothing, as if waiting for a confession on my part, a promise too. I kept my silence, and they answered me with silence. We began conversing in the language of silence. When I understood their silence, I felt that I needed to tell them something more, so I finished off my short silence with a longer silence. When it seemed to me that they understood me, they began asking questions with their eyes, and I couldn't answer them in the same language, as my tear-ducts were out of commission. In the end I relented and said: ""Sorry, I shouldn't have run out alone and barefoot. I promise that tomorrow I'll wear shoes."

"No need for that," Aunt Elizabeth replied, stroking my head: "Didn't you know, sweetheart, people don't usually wear shoes in bed."

For three weeks I was confined to bed. And all this time – as a gesture of solidarity and quite spontaneously – the cows stopped giving milk, the sheep refused to go to pasture, and even the hens gave up laying eggs.

When I travelled to my aunt's farm, the acacia was still in bloom. When I returned, fallen leaves covered the paving stones.

And so melted away, at the first bite, the happiness of that summer in the country.

NINETEEN

The first evening descended on us in Bergen-Belsen. There was darkness in the heart and outside it too. Glowering skies swayed above us. The moon, whose turn it was to light our way, hadn't showed up for the night-shift, and the stars had gone to play with another planet. The hill of depression, on whose summit we had stood for more than four hours, collapsed all at once.

As Pitzi Kleinmann sank to the bottom of the cess-pit, the house of illusions of the last of the optimists was blown apart, and all its tenants dispersed to the four winds.

Eva Waldmann was sobbing quietly, bemoaning her future which henceforward would be shrouded in mist, with the departure of the greatest of clairvoyants. Her son Ziggy didn't know what was going on in her heart, and he didn't understand why she was crying. With the sixth sense of a child he turned to his mother: "Mum, don't cry. I'll give you one of my dolls. Play with Snow White for a while, and you'll feel better."

Exhausted, we arrived at Hut Number 10, which from this

day onward was to be our permanent residence. My mother's face was covered in cold sweat and her hands shook, as if she was suffering from Parkinson's disease. For four solid hours she had been shielding Dad from the inquisitive eye of General Hund, supporting him with the last of her strength, lest he fall.

Suddenly, from one of the dark corners of the hut, a soft musical voice crept into our ears: "Come beloved, to greet the bride, let us welcome the Shabbas." "It's Friday today," said another voice from the shadows, and the Shabbas anthem rang out clearly: "Keep and remember the Shabbas, as the Lord who is one has instructed us in one saying." And all the residents of the hut replied in chorus: "To greet the Shabbas let us go, for it is the source of blessing."

When we had finished eating the tepid liquid called hot soup, in which a few slices of turnip drifted as they pleased, I uttered the jubilant cry: "Glorious soup! I wish we could get to taste it every day!" And God, apparently taking a break from His many other activities, heard my prayer and answered it. From that day onward we were blessed with soup. Our hosts were at pains to nourish us with lunches and suppers composed of one course: deliciously flavoured soup, made from turnips. Every day the same soup, twice daily with love. As for the soup itself, the menu was quite varied. On the lunchtime menu, the soup was listed as a first course, whereas on the supper menu, soup was the main course. The menu being so huge, there was no room for other courses. In the mornings, those eligible were allocated a crust of dry bread with a tiny portion of jam. One of the residents of the hut, who had formerly been a renowned stamp-collector, had managed to bring a magnifying-glass with him. This miraculous instrument was seen as a great boon by the residents and it passed from hand to hand, as a means of locating the precise location of the jam on the latrine shovel, on which the Jews were served their rations.

Mum imposed special routines on the family. Every day we ate two breakfasts: morning breakfast and evening breakfast. In the morning we all ate our portions of bread and jam, and in the evening she surprised us with an extra portion. When we asked where she had got it from, she invented various stories, which all sounded highly implausible.

"I steal an extra portion, without the Germans noticing," she told us, blushing – she and the very concept of theft being poles apart.

"It's true you're stealing, Mum," I answered her – "but it's yourself you're stealing from."

"You're talking nonsense!" she scolded me. "Any more of that, and you'll be turning your mother into a criminal in the eyes of all the family." And she changed the subject abruptly, forgetting that it was she herself who invented the story of theft.

And once again we settled down for the night.

Sleeping arrangements consisted of two-storey bunk beds. Of our family of five, I was the only one assigned to the upper storey. My sister slept on the level below me. Mum, Dad and

Grandpa all slept on the ground-floor.

I climbed onto my bunk and couldn't sleep.

Someone switched on the dark, and utter blackness settled on our quarters. The darkness of Egypt descended on a German hut populated by Jews. Here and there futile attempts were made to bite chunks out of the darkness with the aid of matches, but the tiny flames recoiled, intimidated, from the Stygian gloom and were extinguished the moment they were lit. The darkness was so absolute, even the blind could have seen it.

All were stretched out on their beds, communing with the darkness. The bunks resembled an unfinished flower-bed, which God had covered with a carpet of withered stalks. Voices rose in the void, sometimes colliding and shattering over the heads of the sleepers, those who were so tired they didn't even notice the shower of sounds raining down on them.

"I want to talk to you, answer me if you're awake," a voice addressed its neighbour.

"Of course I'm awake! How could anyone sleep after what we've been through," came the reply. These were the voices of Judith and Tommy, the children of Isaac Rosenfeld, who had fallen during the trek to Bergen-Belsen and been left behind with his precious account-book, the credit sales "charged to God".

"How can it be that God abandoned our father, Tommy?" she asked.

"What else do you expect? Seeing that the Spirit of God has

abandoned God Himself!" he replied bitterly. "But our Daddy was such a saintly man," Judith continued, as if staring helplessly into the incomprehensible – "keeping the commandments, giving secretly to charity, a wonderful family man, kind and courteous – so how do you explain this, Tommy, how?"

"It seems God isn't that keen on saints, or the kind and courteous types either. It's as if people with the kind of qualities our father had are just plain boring to Him. God got fed up with having to listen three times a day to all that sycophantic flannel Dad used to heap on Him in his prayers: there is none like our Lord, none like our King, none like our Saviour... He just got bored stuff, cut off the connection with our Dad" – Tommy concluded his brief sermon.

"But isn't God kind and merciful and forgiving, and all those things?" Judith persisted.

"That's what Dad used to tell Him all the time, but since God is never wrong, it must have been Dad's mistake," said Tommy, tones of weariness creeping into his voice.

"Will you go on believing in God, Tommy?" she asked hesitantly.

"What I'm going to believe in now – sister dear – is a good night's kip," he replied and fell asleep.

Dad was writhing in agony, complaining of unbearable stomach pains. Mum sat beside him, stroking his forehead with one hand, and kneading his stomach with the other. Dad was weak and pale, and lacking the will to contend with his pains.

"Irenika, you're so stubborn, do you know that? Why do you persist in forcing me to stay alive? You should concentrate on looking after the children, not bother yourself with someone who's a living corpse. Can't you see, I'm more dead than alive?"

It was clear that Dad's words were spoken in mental as well as physical anguish. He wanted to say more, but Mum interrupted him:

"Imre, you're talking nonsense. The worst is already behind us, and you'll get through this, you'll see. You've passed harder tests than this in your time. The war will be over soon and there'll be a general amnesty. They'll forgive us for being Jews, we'll be let out of prison and we'll return to our homes in peace. We'll have to brace ourselves, my dear, for all the joys and celebrations that are in store for us, beginning on the threshold of our house and ending who knows where. And our son is going to be Bar-Mitzvah, and our little girl will be starting school, in Class A. You were so happy when she was born, a pretty child with curly, flaxen hair. You laughed until you cried when you saw our son standing by the chimney of the maternity hospital, and waiting for a stork to bring him a sister. You remember how he kept running out into the yard, and whenever he saw a stork landing on one of the roofs, he'd shout at the top of his voice: Mum, come quickly, there's a stork here, ask him to bring me a sister. I always had to try hard not to laugh, and I used to tell him to wait for another stork, a bigger and stronger one, so we'd be sure he wouldn't drop the baby on the way to the hospital. Do you remember the night that the "stork" idea took on a physical shape, and we were frolicking into the small hours of the morning, and our son thought there had been an earthquake that night? We wept with laughter, and when he asked us why we were crying, that set us off again. He wanted to be like us, and he didn't know whether he was supposed to laugh or cry.

"Imre, do you remember those days? They will return, you'll see. I see the big cutting-table waiting for you, and you standing behind it with your tongue hanging out, cutting whole kilometres of material unreeling from the other side of the table. The sewing-machines will be working again, and the hum of their motors will revive our spirits. And when you arrive at the 'Golden Bull', your partners at Table 10 will be waiting for you, and you'll still lose most of the games, because Robbie Friedmann deals you lousy cards, and at midday I'll send our son to call you home for lunch, and you'll turn up at midnight, worn out, and I'll pull off your shoes, and put your head on the pillow, and forgive you, as I always do, for being just a little late…"

Dad suddenly stopped moaning, and Mum was convinced she'd succeeded in healing his pains.

TWENTY

"Happy Purim, happy Purim!" the Jews greeted one another, and their backyards were crowded with fancy-dress clowns. Their faces were radiant and happy, but deep in their hearts all knew that the happiness was part of the make-believe. Their hands were overloaded with musical instruments, producing a riot of sounds: rattles, trumpets, flutes and drums, all kinds of mouth-organs – and whatever came to hand. Even the lids of rusty saucepans served as improvised cymbals.

At that time plague was raging in the town, with the sons of Haman roaming there in herds. If the clowns had blown a fanfare of joy and jubilation on their horns, the walls of the wicked city would have fallen like the walls of Jericho and buried beneath them the sons of Haman. But God had other ideas; no fanfare was heard and the walls did not fall.

In the days leading up to the festival, I was wound up to a high pitch of excitement. At Purim, I was traditionally destined for great things, as Mum used to engineer a central and prestigious role for me, and it was from her that I earned my appointment as "ambassador" for one day, representing the family in many other local homes. The delivery of Purim gifts was an errand laid entirely on my narrow shoulders. Between morning and evening I used to carry out some fifteen to twenty double missions – double because naturally, most of the recipients would repay us with counter-gifts.

A few days before the start of the festival, Mum would devote all her efforts to the serious business of baking. In the community of housewives her status was unassailable, and she had even earned the honorific title of "High Priestess of Jewish cuisine."

Despite the unlimited trust placed in me by Mum, not to mention the great honour that I had been allotted with my appointment to "family ambassador", the food-cupboard and the bakery supplies were strictly out of bounds to me. The most secure part of our house was the larder, where all the ingredients in Mum's baked creations became acquainted with one another: the nuts, the poppies, the cheeses, raisins and all the other sweet things. The larder was kept firmly closed, and even the keys were locked away in a secret place; since my last incursion into this fortress, my assault on the sweetmeats shelf and total annihilation of the ingredients, before they got to see the smallest piece of dough – Mum had decided on a policy of total secrecy regarding their whereabouts.

My love of cakes was insatiable. Whenever the aroma of baking rose to my nostrils, I clung to Mum's apron as I was myself a sticky lump of dough. Aware of this weakness of mine, she would let me lick out all the pans and the dishes where the mixture had been temporarily accommodated on its way to the baking oven, until there was no need to clean them any more, since I hadn't left behind the tiniest morsel of poppy, or a fragment of anything else.

When the longed-for day arrived and the joy of Purim erupted within the walls of sad houses, I put on my ambassador's uniform. Two trays laden with cheese and poppy cakes were handed to me as a temporary deposit; the nut and apple cakes awaited their turn with appropriate patience. Confronted by the exhilarating spectacle appearing before me, the void of my mouth filled with gushing secretions, and it seemed that a narrow cascade of spittle was beginning to make its way towards the trays.

"Shut your mouth!" Mum shouted. "You're dribbling on the cakes."

"It's not my fault," I defended myself – "I'm leaking at all corners."

"Then we'll have to fill your mouth with something solid, to stop the dribbling."

Exactly as I had hoped, Mum lined my mouth thoroughly, stuffing me with poppy cakes as if I was a fowl being fattened for the table, until the dripping stopped altogether.

With the measured gait of an "ambassador" I strode towards the first destination. To my right my mother walked and to my left, my little sister. For the first and second errands there was a kind of fixed ritual; my mother would insist on accompanying me to be sure the cakes arrived at their destination. Her concern over my proclivities, and my ability to withstand temptation, was outweighed by another fear – of a wolf in disguise intercepting me, snatching away the tray of sweetmeats and marring the joy of the festival.

My sister was dressed up as Snow White, and instead of dwarves she held in her hand seven coloured balloons.

As we walked our regular route, to the house of my grandpa on my father's side, a gang of youths leapt out from one of the alleyways. Some six ruffians – teenagers dressed in the uniform of the "Crossbow" movement – blocked our path.

"Look at this, look at this," their leader turned to the others with an ostentatious sneer of contempt. "The fat Jew woman is at it again, smuggling contraband for the black market – and in wartime too!"

"The penalty for smuggling is a bullet in the head," one of the gang members added.

The way they were discussing us – conversation flowing between them as if of its own accord – we might just as well not have been there.

Mum didn't lose her composure. Signalling to me not to provoke the ruffians, she pushed us back and stood between us and the gang. Sounding calm and serene, she addressed the "Crossbow" youths:

"Gentlemen, we're not smuggling anything at all. What you have here is a law-abiding citizen, out walking for pleasure with her two little children, so please let us carry on our way."

"You see, Peter," – one of the thugs turned to the leader, still with his back turned to Mum – "you're abusing a peaceful and law-abiding citizen, and accusing her of the serious crime of smuggling. Don't you think you owe her an apology, Peter?" And at that very moment he executed a sharp turn, spinning his head round to face Mum, and spat forcefully on her left cheek.

"And what will you say now, stinking Jewess? Will you say it's raining? Then brace yourself for the flood!" This was the signal for the start of the onslaught on Mum. It began with spitting – jets of saliva hitting her from every mouth – and then they butted her in the stomach like prancing bulls, until they knocked her to the ground. My sister was scared, and the balloons were scared too, flying from her hands and going straight up to Heaven. Miraculously, the thugs didn't notice the pair of trays that I'd put down at the edge of the pavement. I snuggled with my sister against my mother's chest to protect her, and we waited for the next wave. But it didn't come. The exhilarated assailants left the scene of battle, the crown of heroes returning from the killing fields resplendent on their heads. I didn't say a word. I'd learned from Mum to weep in the heart, and when the heart weeps, the lips are tightly sealed.

Mum felt acute pains in all parts of her body, but didn't complain. Her coiffured hair was dishevelled and hung in clumps over her bruised forehead. The colour of her face was ruddy grey. The gold of her body blended with the gold of the earth.

Big drops of rain, each the size of a tear, began falling from the sky. I didn't know if God was weeping, or sweating for shame.

"How are you feeling, children?" she asked suddenly, as if we were sitting by the fireside in our living room at home, and holding out both hands to us she said: "Come on, my dears, I want to give you a kiss." She kissed us both, leaving a stain behind on our foreheads. The colour of the stain was ruddy grey.

Suddenly I saw that the two trays had been overturned, and the cakes strewn over the pavement. My instinct was to gobble them up, but I restrained myself. I gathered them together without my mother noticing, and put them on the tray in a different order.

I remembered Purim of the year before. After two rounds of obligatory errands, I was absolutely independent; that year, I wasn't even accompanied by my sister. On the way to my aunt's house, Aunt Elizabeth the Second, I had to cut across the empty lot on the corner where we used to play football. I was sure that at Purim I wouldn't find a living soul there, as all the children must have been drafted into running errands. As it turned out I was mistaken. The pitch was swarming with children, and the moment they saw me with the trays, they broke into peals of raucous laughter. Willy, the class ruffian, was there too, conferring with his retinue of sycophants. When he caught sight of me he pointed a finger at me, and this was the signal for collective assault. The children pounced on me and snatched away the two trays, then sat down in a circle and with ravenous appetite, proceeded to gobble up all the cakes that my mother had baked, decorated and packed, so they would arrive fresh and tasty on the table of Aunt Elizabeth the Second. I was aghast, and utterly at a loss. I was about to attack Willy, by way of retaliation, when someone pointed to a big pile behind my back. It was a stack of trays which, on their way to various dining-rooms, had got struck in the football field, just like my trays. As it became clear later, Willy had been behind the whole caper; he thought up, planned and executed the Great Cake Robbery.

When the deliveries failed to arrive, many households were cast into deep dudgeon, deprived of the opportunity to enjoy their traditional Purim fare – choice cakes prepared by the sorceresses of Jewish cuisine.

Like fire in a field of thorns, the rumour spread that back-yard altercations had disrupted the festival deliveries, or per-haps the omens had been bad – such as the sighting of a black cat in the wrong place. No one imagined that this wasn't a case of evil genies escaping from the community's bottle, but was simply down to the mischief of a certified scamp.

I wondered what was going on in Willy's mind. With all the courage I could muster, I invited him to join me for a confi-dential chat. I surprised myself with the tactic I had adopted and another, bigger surprise was in store for me – Willy's acceptance of my invitation.

We moved away to the far end of the pitch, and for a while fought a duel of looks.

"Why are you doing this, Willy?" I asked, opting for the brusque and direct approach.

"Why am I doing what?" he countered, predictably.

"Oh come on, don't play the innocent!" I protested.

We sat down on a heap of earth, and I couldn't believe what I saw then. Willy pulled out a cigarette from some secret pocket in his clothing, stuck it between his lips and, like an actor in a smoking commercial, lit it nonchalantly, and a moment later was already blowing out perfect smoke-rings.

I sat staring at him open-mouthed, frozen, like a puppet hung on a hook after the show.

"I bet you're surprised," he said, opening all the apertures in his face, to expel the smoke.

"You know when I started smoking? At seven years old. I learnt it from my Dad, and he was addicted to tobacco like a baby's addicted to his mother's tits. My Dad never used matches, he lit the next cigarette from the last one. When he popped out of his mother's womb, he had a fag in his mouth. Anything else in the world he could do without – only not the pleasure of smoking. When the cigarette factory in town caught fire and there was a serious shortage of cigs, he was wandering around in a trance. You couldn't even talk to him, until he heard one of the local tobacconists had a secret cache hidden away. In the dead of night he broke into that store-room and grabbed every last packet, left the place empty."

Willy suddenly halted the flow of his story, tightened his lips around the burning cigarette and drew a double dose of smoke into his lungs. I reckoned I saw a slight tremor setting his whole body on edge.

"You know?" he continued slowly in a lower tone, a note of cynicism creeping into his voice. "My Dad did have one other pleasure in life. He loved beating, and most of all he love beating my Mum and me. Any excuse, and he'd raise that long arm of his and whack me and my Mum around the head, so hard it seemed like all the bells in all the churches had started ringing all at once. The daily menu of quarrels between Mum and Dad was rich and varied – and there was always violence for dessert. As long as I can remember, and that isn't long, my memories are of one long cycle of violence. The photograph album of my childhood is the record of my father's resounding love for his only son.

"Sometimes, and only sometimes, in the interval between one series of blows and the next, when he was in a forgiving mood, he used to sit me on his knee and teach me things that seemed important to him. That's how I learned to smoke. I was just a little kid and he used to yell at me: 'I'm going to beat you till I make a man out of you.' Then one day he took the burning cigarette out of his mouth and shoved it between my lips and said: 'Be a man and take a little drag of this. No one's died of smoking yet.' I took a little drag and nearly choked on it. Dad stopped beating me soon after that. He died of lung cancer."

For a long time we sat on the dust pile, in silence, Willy wreathing my head with a garland of smoke.

All the way I was thinking about Mum's cakes, that I'd picked up from the pavement.

When we arrived at Grandpa's house, all let out sighs of relief. Grandpa asked why we were late, and we invented a plausible excuse. He went on to say that they were all waiting impatiently for Mum's famous poppy cakes, and moments later the trays were snatched from my hands. I decided this was my cue to disappear. From my hiding-place under the sofa, I watched as all the guests swooped on Mum's poppy cakes, and after the first bite I noticed how the assembled company had divided into two camps: those who screwed up their faces, and those whose faces turned pale. All alike stood awkwardly, mouths full, unable to swallow and too shy to spit out.

Grandpa, a man not renowned for his tact, turned to Mum and asked her in a loud voice: "Irenika, what's the matter with you this year? What were you thinking of, putting *salt* in the poppy cakes – and at Purim too!"

When Mum started looking for me, I was praying hard, asking God to turn me into a pillar of salt.

TWENTY ONE

After four weeks of living in Bergen-Belsen, eternity seemed a temporary phenomenon compared with the sense of infinitude that the camp imposed on its inmates and prisoners. Suffering became routine, routine became a plague, and it's in the nature of plague to leave casualties. The Germans arrested all hopes and crucified them, as once they crucified Jesus. Even yearnings went underground. All the dreams that we tried to smuggle out of the camp were caught and hung on the electric fence, for all to see.

One morning, on rising, my five year old sister asked Mum when she would be starting in Class A.

"When you finish at the nursery," Mum told her.

"So I'm in the nursery now?" she went on to ask – "So why aren't there any toys here? And why doesn't the nursery teacher ever tell me stories? I love hearing stories. And if I had a little doll I could take her to the playground and sit with her on a rocking horse, and rock with her all day long, until the horse says: That's enough! I don't want to rock any more, I'm tired, I want to sleep."

Mum wrapped herself in her favourite headscarf, the red one, that even Dad liked to see her wearing. She pulled out a few rags that had been kept hidden under her bunk, and there and then improvised a pretty doll, with two red plaits. She told me to go down on all fours and put my sister, with her doll, on my back, and as she rocked them, with my active assistance, she began telling them a story:

"Once upon a time there was a little girl, in a faraway country, who went for a walk with her older brother in the big wood. The little girl loved butterflies very much and she asked her brother to catch some for her. When he managed to catch a pretty butterfly, which had two white wings and a lot of red spots, the little girl was very happy and she put the butterfly in a big cardboard box. The white butterfly began to cry, because he couldn't fly away and be free again, however hard he tried. The girl and her brother were enchanted by his bright colours and they decided not to let him go. The butterfly beat his wings in despair against the lid of the box and pleaded for his life. And he said he was supposed to be flying from flower to flower, and he really loved drinking their nectar, and if the girl and her brother wouldn't let him go, he would die in the box, of a broken heart. The flowers would be sad, and wither, and if he didn't get to them soon they too would die of sorrow."

My sister was much moved by the story, and she asked Mum to talk to the girl and her brother and persuade them to release the trapped butterfly. Mum told her there was no need for these, because the girl herself realised she was doing something she shouldn't.

"And then the little girl took the cardboard box in her hands," – Mum continued with her story – "and she began singing happy songs in honour of the butterfly, and very very slowly she opened the box and said to him: 'Fly away, white butterfly, fly to the lovely flowers in the wood and dance your butterfly dance for them.' The white butterfly came out of the box, clapped his wings together, to say thank you, and because he was very thirsty, he flew straight to the flowers in the big wood, and sucked their nectar until he wasn't thirsty any more."

And I said to Mum: "Mum, that's enough! I don't want to rock any more, I'm tired and I want to sleep."

In the night I heard my sister talking in her dream: "I hope God doesn't punish the girl and her brother. I hope God will forgive them." Then she fell asleep.

Next morning, at first light, the guards stormed into Hut 10, their loud yells ripping us away from the world of illusions. We were ordered to muster on the parade ground within three minutes. It was bitterly cold in the hut, cold enough to set the skin tingling. The percussion band – chattering teeth – launched into the dawn concert, under the presiding baton of the great white chill. Clothes were grabbed hastily, lest they be forfeited on account of some unexpected delay: late arrivals on parade could expect punishments liable to endanger their health, punishments which involved spending the whole night tied up outside, in the freezing snow.

From a distance we had already caught sight of the high platform set up on the parade ground, and the gibbet towering above it.

I don't know where we found the strength of mind and body – confronted as we were by the optical illusions of extreme temperatures, turning human beings into blocks of ice – to stand in straight lines on the parade ground, straighter than any line ever drawn with a ruler. For a long time we stood in the piercing cold, struggling not to be turned into pillars of ice.

It was only after an exhausting wait that General Hund appeared, wrapped in a fur coat and accompanied by his minions.

He mounted the stage, his eyes flashing sparks of hatred, and began his speech with a long and ominous silence.

"Listen you, scum of the human race!" – the General was as civil as ever – "Last night something serious happened, something unpardonable. We have received information from the celebrated German Intelligence Service, that property of the Third Reich has been stolen and misappropriated. From the stocks of turnips – fodder for cattle and for Jews – *two* turnips have been stolen! The contemptible insect who broke into the turnip store failed to take into account the fact that the Third Reich conducts thorough checks of its stores, at least twice a day. Needless to say, the swine has been apprehended, and this very morning will receive the appropriate punishment."

General Hund snapped two fingers of his right hand, and

all the frozen company flinched. A boy, no more than a child, was pushed onto the platform with hands tied, as naked as the day he was born. When his face was revealed, Mum hastily put her hand over my lips, to stifle the howl of anguish that I was about to utter.

The boy who, driven by hunger, thought he could outwit the Third Reich, was Willy.

Like trapped water breaking free of its restraints, floods of memories washed over me, wave upon wave: the Great Cake Robbery of the Purim before last, followed by the heart-to-heart conversation that demolished the barriers between us, and suddenly I was straining my ears to hear the famous derogatory song that the choir used to sing under Willy's direction: "Tommy Langer is a fool, clowns around all day in school…" and then I realised I would no longer have a rival in the sprint races, no one pretending to collapse on the running track thirty metres short of the finishing line – because Willy was setting out now on the longest run of all. He'd be competing in races in Heaven, contests which only true champions are eligible to enter.

The cold seeped into our bones, as Willy stood like a crag defying the winds, staring the Third Reich full in the eye, and the Third Reich stuffed a turnip into his mouth and tightened the noose around his neck.

And then the prisoners saw God's image swinging in the wind, this way and that, back and forth, back and forth…

I wanted to tell God something but I couldn't, as Mum's hand was still clamped over my mouth.

TWENTY TWO

During the many social visits paid to our house by Robbie Friedmann, Dad's regular partner at Table 10 in the "Golden Bull" he was always asking my mother: "Well, how is Toscanini? And whenever Robbie asked this question, Mum used to call me, because I was Toscanini. In his status as an honorary member of the household, Robbie used to come and go without any need for formal invitations.

In the course of his prolonged visits to us, he made it his regular habit to "catch" me in odd situations. I for my part – with a fair degree of frequency – used to pick up a stick resembling a baton, climb on a high chair and conduct the bubbles of the air, as if they were musicians in a big orchestra, and Robbie would put his lips close to Mum's ear and whisper softly, not wanting to disrupt the performance: "You see, Irenika? You've got a little Toscanini growing up here.

After the umpteenth such whisper, the name of Toscanini began to permeate Mum's consciousness. One day, when I came home from school, she sat me on her knee, and said she was going to tell me about Toscanini. I asked her politely if it tasted sweet or bitter, and Mum explained to me that Toscanini wasn't a brand of chocolate. She was well aware that I didn't like bitter chocolate.

After a while she bought me a proper conductor's baton, and I conducted everything that moved. I used to run to the yard carrying a little stool, set it up before the margosa tree and stand on it, to the sound of the applause of the leaves. When I raised the baton in the air, the tree fell silent, and then the orchestra of the leaves launched into the "Wind Symphony", conducted by Arturo Toscanini. And so I moved from tree to tree, conducting all the famous compositions of the natural world. As my reputation spread, I received invitations to conduct in other settings too, and that's how I got to visit the concert-halls of the local poultry farmers, conducting the choir of the fledgling chicks. Every time the curtain came down on a stirring performance, I would return home hovering in an acoustic haze. One evening, in a state of particular exhilaration, I took a big pair of scissors and liberated the feathers that padded my quilt. As the feathers drifted aimlessly in the void, I waved my baton again, to conduct the soft sounds that were caressing me inside and out.

In my bed at night, before sleeping, I used to dream of conducting, and by the time I was entangled in the web of sleep, I was already conducting in my dream. I dreamt that all the orchestras in the town had united to form one big philharmonia, and I was conducting it in Dari Square, to the delight of thousands of cheering listeners.

Unfortunately, I tended to wake up in mid-concert, and I would ask Mum why she couldn't postpone her "Good morning" until the end of the performance. My astonished mother, having no answer to this question, used to put her hand on my forehead, to check that I wasn't feverish.

Despite the close ties of friendship between my parents and Robbie Friedmann, they never visited his bachelor apartment. Mum was curious to know details of his living conditions, this man of so many faces. How many rooms does his "dacha" comprise? What is his taste in furniture and what colour are his curtains? Does he have a bath, or just a shower, and are his carpets wall-to-wall? And his wardrobe – naturally this interested Mum especially.

Shrouded in mystery was how the figure of Robbie Friedmann seemed, and it was almost impossible to speculate about his activities without encountering some major paradoxes. Having heard so much about him at home, I found my parents' curiosity, my mother's in particular, infectious.

One day, early in the evening when the local football pitch was wrapped in a thick blanket of dusk and the rag-ball we were playing with had turned black, I deviated from my usual homeward route and walked up the street like a robot, guided by remote-control to a certain destination. After a while I found myself facing an ancient gate, which stood like a superannuated sentry at the entrance to a single storey apartment-house. The cold handle, stuck in the mouth of the door like an extinguished pipe, responded to my steady pressure and a narrow aperture appeared, through which I slipped cautiously and quietly.

Having passed through the gate, I found myself in a big and empty courtyard, slumped in its evening drowsiness. During the day the courtyard served as a social centre for the tenants of the apartments dispersed around it; it was both a children's playground and a gossip-exchange for the adults. I walked along the inner path, lit by the faint lights of the houses, filtering through closed windows sealed by thick curtains. When I reached the last in the line of apartments on the western side of the yard, I felt my heart-rate quicken.

I was standing in the doorway of Robbie Friedmann's house. The light emerging from the window of his house looked paler than the lights from the other apartments. Standing in the yard, I couldn't think of a good explanation for this strange phenomenon, and I decided that the puzzle had to be solved from the inside. I knocked on the door three times and no answer came. I pressed the handle and much to my surprise, the door swung open quite obediently.

I found myself in a dark vestibule, leading directly into a lounge of considerable size, with no partition in between. A strange atmosphere enveloped the apartment, as if it was trapped inside a bubble of mystery. The room was suffused with candle-light, and this accounted for the difference in the level of illumination visible from outside. Robbie was totally unaware of my presence. He sat at a square table in the middle of the room, a very festive looking table, set for two diners. In the middle stood two candlesticks, with a pair of white candles poking flamboyant fiery tongues in his direction.

Robbie was wearing black evening dress; under the jacket was a gleaming white starched shirt, with armlets to hold the sleeves in place. A red bow-tie encircled his neck, and a handkerchief of the same colour was tucked in his upper pocket. The gramophone played soft background music, blending nicely with the romantic atmosphere enfolding the room. Robbie sat by the table like a groom, awaiting his bride of the evening. He seemed relaxed, not glancing even once at his watch, or turning to look in the direction of the door, as is usual when an important guest is expected.

The only extraordinary thing about the room's décor was a big mannequin doll, one of those that stand in store windows and change their clothes according to the dictates of fashion and the season. The doll stood not far from the table, stark naked. Entranced by the sound of the music emerging from the gramophone, Robbie began humming the tune softly, while taking an occasional sip of his favourite wine. Then he rose from his seat, calmly changed the record, and to the strains of a romantic South American tango, he approached the naked model, bowed to her ceremoniously and invited her to dance. Seeing that she raised no objection, he took the doll in his arms, whispered words of gratitude in her ear, and began dancing with her to the sensuous rhythm of the tango. Robbie emptied whole bucketfuls of love over his be-loved, such as no store-front model had ever bathed in before. Before they moved on to dance the waltz, he placed a garland of red roses on her head and kissed himself on her behalf, in token of gratitude. The pair stood up on the tips of their toes, and I found myself conducting Tchaikovsky's "Swan Lake", as interpreted, unconventionally, by Robbie Friedmann and a store-front dummy.

When Robbie told my parents about his passionate affair with a top model, who was also a renowned ballet dancer, and said he wished he could find some way of evading her clutches, I sealed my lips and slipped out of the room on tiptoe, as if I was a ballet-dancer myself.

It was only then that I understood why Robbie was such a sought-after guest at virgins' conventions, and an honorary member of the married ladies' guild too.

TWENTY THREE

When Dad had stopped moaning with the pain, he closed his eyes and fell into a deep sleep. His breathing stabilised, the curling wrinkles that furrowed his forehead seemed to have straightened by themselves, and even the craters of weariness gaping in his face were filled with calm. The light and mischievous smile that used to animate his features in the past, that had faded into nothing in recent times, came back to adorn once again his attractive features. His smooth and bare head reminded many of the beautiful and hidden side of the moon. Suddenly he held out his hand to me and said abruptly: "Come with me, my boy, let's go on a trip together." Hand in hand we crossed the frontier of dreams, needing no visas or passports, and I was stuck close to him, as a *mezuzah* sticks to a door.

In the dream we were sitting in a big bare expanse, with mountains enclosing it all around, rising to a pinnacle as high as the vault of the sky. The whole of the plain was strewn with little stones, sprouting from the ground in disciplined strips, like lines of dwellings waiting for settlers. The name of the plain was "Hall of Creation", and in the foreground stood a smooth platform, serving as a stage for performances. We sat by ourselves in the "hall", in the best seats in the middle, and saw angels dancing before us. This was the dance-display troupe of the angels of Heaven, putting on a special matinee performance in Dad's honour. Like gazelles the angels soared above the stage, never touching it with their feet, and between one dance and the next they went up to Heaven to change their costumes. Sometimes they danced in white garb, sometimes in black and back again, until the interval. Dad noticed that in the last dance before the interval the angels were dressed in black, so he was expecting the first dance after the interval to be performed in white. But no: the troupe climbed down the long ladder from Heaven still wearing the same costume, and so the angels danced on to the end of the show, without changing their black garments.

All this time Mum sat at Dad's bedside, watching his calm face, monitoring his steady breathing and travelling to the end of personal memory. She wasn't separated for a moment from the red scarf, wrapped around the upper part of her body and affording partial protection from the intense cold which mocked and disdained the thin walls of Hut 10.

Mum saw that the coloured ball – which she'd been given not long before, a present from her father – was intent on rolling away down the corridor. In a flash a frantic race was under way between the ball and my mother; which would arrive

first at the edge of the slope above the looming chasm? Mum
chased after the ball, skipping like a light-limbed antelope,
in the attempt to overtake it before it could make its suicidal
leap…

That year, the year 1925, an early spring tempted the girls
to go out into the bosom of nature. My mother was no excep-
tion, joining her friends in their quest, their desire to walk
across the bridge linking winter with summer. In keeping
with the colours of the season, the girls wore white, and their
virginity was crying out to be matched against the virginity of
the spring. Mum's basket was crammed to overflowing with
coils of wool, pledged in marriage to ornate knitting threads,
of all the colours of the rainbow.

…When the mischievous ball sensed my Mum already
breathing down its neck, it quickened its pace and began
bouncing in zigzag fashion, to elude her grasp. She was determined to catch up with it at all costs! Smug and elated,
it sped towards the slope, teasing her with flashes of colour.
Just as the ball thought it had outwitted her, its progress was
blocked and it came to a sudden halt, trapped between a pair
of splayed feet. Mum stopped abruptly too, as if finding her
way barred by a brick wall. All her attention was focused on
the ball, which no longer had any prospect of escape. Very
slowly she raised her head and her eyes met those of a tall
and handsome man. He smiled at her and she blushed. When
he introduced himself, she mumbled something and looked
down. He stooped, picked up the ball and placed it in her
hands. For a long time they held the ball between them, and as

she gazed at his long fingers it was as if she touched electricity, a force releasing currents in her she had never known existed. And then he introduced himself again, and she already knew she was in love with my father. Some time later he put a ring on her finger, and she never removed it all the days of her life.

When seven successive lean years passed by, during which time never – not even once – was the miracle of conception celebrated in my mother's womb, she didn't despair and didn't shut away her hopes. With all her fortitude she waited for the seven prosperous years.

One night when the moon was full and round, she purified her body, her soul as well, and with joyful heart surrendered herself to her pair of lovers, my father and God. While my father was pouring his love into her and bathing in caves of honey, her head was resting in God's lap.

"How is it?" – she asked in a submissive tone – "How is it that the earth is fertile, the tree gives its fruit, and it is only my belly which is fallow, my womb which lies under the curse of barrenness?"

And God heeded her appeal, and despite His longstanding vow, decided to take pity on her. And when the face of the moon turned pale in the third watch of the night, millions of tiny seeds were already besieging her portals. I was the first… making love to my mother's eggs.

Having travelled in spirit to faraway places, Mum was suddenly alarmed to hear my sister's voice, crying: "Rain! Rain!"

All the occupants of the hut were jolted from their sleep and leapt from their bunks, looking for umbrellas. "What's all this about rain?" said Mum, glancing around her. "Everything's dry," she declared, approaching my sister's bunk. She couldn't believe what she was seeing: it wasn't just rain descending on the bunk, it was a positive cloudburst. "What is this, a mirage?" she asked, forgetting for a moment that my bunk was directly above my sister's. The one responsible for the change in the weather was I, urinating on her in my sleep, until the poor creature was almost drowned in the deluge.

Dad, lying on the nearby bunk, smiled broadly from cheek to cheek, and Mum didn't know if he was awake, or smiling in a dream…

TWENTY FOUR

In the house of Kitty, the senior employee in my father's tailoring kingdom, preparations were under way for a double celebration. The fact that the town had been cleansed of its Jewish population was enough in itself to justify shifting the bolts of the wine-cellars and opening their doors to all the thirsty; but if the God of the Jews had a handsome bonus in mind, enabling members of the household to inherit abandoned Jewish property, this called for nothing less than slaying the fatted pig and conducting devout and appropriate sacrifice.

Kitty's house stood on the edge of the town, away from the bustling centre. The house, like most houses of its type, had a large and spacious courtyard, with fruit trees planted at its edges. In the middle of the yard was an ancient oak-tree, its canopy – like an open umbrella – offering shelter to all those who took refuge beneath it, from sun and rain alike.

The trees were linked together with a thick electrical cable, and the leaves were bathed in the flickering light of dozens of coloured bulbs. Above the space occupied by the musicians a big cotton sheet had been unfurled, bearing the painted slogan, in big, eye-catching letters: AT LAST, HUNGARY FOR THE HUNGARIANS!

In a nearby corner – the slaughtered pig corner – tables groaning under the weight of delicacies winked at aficionados of the pig. In the attitude of the Hungarians towards the pig, there was an element of ambiguity. They drew a clear distinction between two types of pig, the Jewish pig, which they detested, and the pedigree pig, with blue porcine blood flowing in his veins, which they admired. Great care was taken to prevent any intermingling between the two breeds – perish the thought! The Jewish pig, for example, was forbidden access to the sty of the pedigree pig. And if the pedigree pig was ever caught fraternising with a Jewish pig, he would be instantly declared taboo – his flesh unfit for ritual sacrifice.

Not far from the slaughtered pig corner, stout barrels of wine had been placed, having enjoyed a prolonged period of gestation. Kitty patrolled the yard like a plump gander, one who knows that all living creatures seek his favour and accept his authority.

Until not so long ago she had been sitting at a machine in Dad's factory, running out strips of material by the kilometre, and marrying them together with gay sewing threads that danced to the rhythm of an anxious needle, rising and falling to the sound of the humming motor. Her eyes expressed humility, and the mark of her obedience was branded on her forehead. Kitty practised iron discipline in her work: no other employee arrived before her in the morning, or left after her in the evening. My parents were very fond of Kitty, and over the years she became a member of the family. She never complained over working conditions, and asked no favours for herself, even obliquely. Any bonuses added to her salary were paid at my father's initiative.

One harsh winter day she rose early as usual, and on her way to the factory she slipped on the icy pavement and broke her right arm. Ten days of rest, she was told by the doctors at the hospital, when her arm had been put in plaster. Kitty couldn't stand the thought of even one day at home; she ignored the doctors' instructions, and the morning after the accident she was already sitting at her sewing machine, fingers peeping out from the roll of plaster. Dad did his best to persuade her to take a few days off, and even threatened to lock her out.

"If you do that," she said – "I'll just sit on the step outside the door until you let me get back to work." Dad knew who he was dealing with, and realising he had no choice, he gave way.

A week before the German army invaded Hungary, my parents came to the conclusion that the Third Reich was not going to leave the country's Jews alone, and until the crisis had passed, some precautionary measures should be taken. My mother ordered a general call-up of her ornaments, a summons obeyed by items of jewellery and trinkets from every drawer, some of them heirlooms passed down through the generations, others added to the treasury over the years at Dad's expense. When all the ornaments had been assembled, Mum stowed them in one big box. At the same time, Dad rolled away the heavy stone covering the entrance to the materials cache, and dozens of rolls were brought up from their underground hiding-place and stowed temporarily in the lounge of our house. After a brief discussion between my parents, they decided on the next step that the circumstances required, and the following day, Kitty was asked to stay behind for an extra hour. At the end of the working day, when all the other employees had left, Kitty was invited into the house to discuss an issue of importance. Obedient and submissive as ever, she sat on the very edge of the armchair – half of her backside suspended in the air – all her body-language an eloquent expression of humility and modest expectations.

"Kitty my dear," – Dad turned to her when all had finished drinking the tea Mum had provided – "these are hard times for us Jews, and God only knows what is in store for us. You know how fond we are of you, and how much we appreciate your loyalty to our family. For almost ten years we have been meeting every day and spending a third of our lives together. We have come to know you inside and out, and with your integrity and reliability you have earned our unlimited trust. There's no knowing what the future holds, and my wife and I have decided to entrust to you a portion of our property, and ask you to hold it, as a pledge, until the crisis is over. Naturally, we promise you a handsome reward for your efforts." When Dad had finished his speech, he leaned back in his armchair, and absolute silence reigned in the room.

Kitty was stunned, utterly dumbfounded. She put her right hand to her heart, opened her mouth to say something, and no sound came. Her face was the colour of a ripe tomato, and the half of her backside that was perched on the seat slipped gradually forward, nearly joining its partner, suspended in the air. With stupendous effort she succeeded in uttering three words: "But Mister Eisner…" before lapsing again into silence. Minutes dragged on, feeling like hours, until she recovered her composure:

"But Mister Eisner, how can you imagine such a thing? Do you think I need a reward for looking after your property? Of course I'll take care of it. I'll hide everything in a secret place, where no one will find it, where it's going to be safe, and you can be sure you'll get everything back that you entrusted to me, intact and undamaged. I'm delighted to know that you're relying on me, and I feel honoured to be doing you this small service. And it may be there'll be no need for it anyway. The war will be over soon and the Jews will once again be full citizens of Hungary, with all their civil rights restored."

That very night a large proportion of the family's property was transferred to Kitty's house.

Two days later, 19 March 1944, Hitler's armies invaded Hungary. That day, Kitty once again stayed behind to work overtime, but on this occasion all the others stayed with her. At the end of the day, in an ostentatious manner, Kitty stripped from her face the mask of ten years, exposing a pair of green eyes flashing hatred. For ten years my parents had been looking into this face, never realising that what they were seeing was a mask.

While my flabbergasted father was trying to digest the change, Kitty shouted at him: "Hey you, d'you hear me?" My father looked around him, wondering who was being addressed in this manner.

Kitty rose from her seat, her over-inflated bust jutting out proudly, and with an expression of sheer glee, began shooting her poisoned arrows: "Take a look at Baron Shitface, pretending he doesn't hear and doesn't understand!" The workers set about their business like a disciplined and well-drilled team. Within minutes they had made a broad circle with their bodies, and as if we were performing monkeys in a circus ring, they led the four of us into the middle of the circle, sat us on tall chairs, and with broad smiles plastered on their faces, sewed eye-catching yellow patches on our chests – twice the size required by regulations.

An unending stream of guests poured into the courtyard of Kitty's house. All were in festive attire, but standing out above the rest in sartorial terms was Kitty's husband, wearing an elegantly tailored suit, made from cloth of the very finest quality and smelling faintly of mothballs. The party was in full swing and people strolled about the yard in high spirits. Wine flowed like water, and waiters filled the guests' goblets, time after time, with the world's most famous vintage – Hungarian tokay. The most favoured corner of all, predictably, was the pig's corner. The band played rousing reels and quick-steps, and between dances bellies were stuffed full, their walls lined with layer after layer of succulent pork. At the height of the festivities, Kitty silenced the musicians and mounted the podium like a glorious peacock, all radiant with happiness and smiling broadly. With an elegant movement, she opened her handbag and drew out a sheet of white paper. Now, with all the spotlights turned on her and all eyes focused on her small figure, encased in a black party-frock, the guests were dazzled by the sparkling jewellery that adorned her neck and other exposed parts of her body. Like water breaking on a thirsty beach, wave upon wave, the golden lights swamped the eyes of the women, and there were gasps and exclamations of wonder at the splendour of her accoutrements.

"Guests and friends," Kitty began, reading from her script – "today is a festival. Although this is a festival that does not yet appear in our calendar, it is our duty to celebrate it henceforward and forever. I hereby declare that this day is a festival of thanksgiving to the Good Lord, who has purged our land of the Jewish parasites, suckers of the blood of the Hungarian people. Let us raise our glasses and drink a toast to the great nation of Hungary, which at last belongs to Hungarians alone."

The crowd applauded her and cried "Hurrah!" three times, waving their glasses in the air and pouring the wine into their stomachs, in the wake of the pioneering pig.

When Kitty descended from the stage and was again engulfed by the throng, there were many who pressed forward, hoping for a closer look at her finery. Out of the crowd heaving about her, one woman plucked up the courage to ask Kitty, in a loud voice, where these jewels had come from.

"Inherited, my dear, inherited," she replied tersely. "I inherited them from my adoptive parents, who died recently in obscure circumstances."

It's a pity I never got to adopt parents like those! – the questioner mused to herself, and hurried away to another party, where a plentiful supply of wine and pork was also guaranteed.

TWENTY FIVE

The last day of the month of January 1945 was one more day of normality on the face of the earth, as if the war of the sons of light and the sons of darkness was taking place on another planet.

In St. Moritz in Switzerland, the skiers again rose early for an extra day on the *piste*. In the fashionable and colourful garb of the ski-enthusiast, they "ploughed" the snow-covered mountains, racing with the light breeze and leaving it far behind. Not everyone who made the pilgrimage to St. Moritz was kitted out for skiing. Many of the pilgrims were tormented by their neutral consciences, and came to cleanse them in the white snow.

The "Jerbeau" café in Budapest – not far from the bank of the Dnuva – was thronged with cheerful café idlers, regular guests, trying to keep to the routine of their day, lest it be diverted from its regular route. Energetic waiters cleared themselves a path, threading their bodies between the loops of smoke hovering above tables laden to overflowing, and served a traditional breakfast, garnished with choice cuts of pork, and for dessert – coffee with honey-cake. Between courses, the men pored over the headlines in the morning papers and stripped the waitresses with their eyes.

At that hour, in New York, the evening lights were on, to guide lovers through the ways of the night. A woman, hemmed in on all sides, dug her nails blissfully into the buttocks of the conqueror. And when the tables were turned, she straddled him in the pose of a professional jockey, rising and falling on his saddle until the horse cried: "Hurrah for conquest!"

Dad went on smiling from cheek to cheek, and Mum paced about the hut numb with grief. He didn't stop smiling even when the gates of the camp were opened, and a cart hitched to two emaciated horses crawled lazily inside, heading in the direction of the parade-ground. The faces of the horses were like the faces of men. Dad lay on the bunk without moving and only smiled. Wrapped in her red scarf, Mum covered the whole expanse of the hut, walking backwards and forwards and biting her nails. The horses towed the cart to a pre-ordained destination, needing no driver to control them. There was something very human about the horses, quite touching. It seemed to Mum that Dad wanted to say something, but he didn't speak, he smiled all the time. She covered her face with both her hands, as if she was about to rend her hair, but had changed her mind. Fifty pairs of eyes were fixed on her. The horses shuffled their hooves in the heavy snow covering the parade ground; the horses seemed to know what they were waiting for.

When Dad was laid on the cart, I thought he was going

to be cold, and soon his face would be twisted into a frozen grimace. But this didn't happen and he just went on smiling. I was afraid he might catch pneumonia, but I didn't dare say anything. I kept silent. A little while later they put someone else beside Dad, someone with a face full of pain, and I was sure this would spoil his mood. It turned out I was wrong here as well, because the smile didn't budge from his face. More people were loaded and when space began running short, they started putting them on top of Dad. I was afraid he was going to suffocate, but then I saw he was still smiling, and I was relieved to know that at least he wouldn't be cold.

When the cart was loaded to the brim, piled high with people, as if in a blind habit of obedience to an order given by remote control – the two horses began pulling the cart towards the gate. Mum picked up my sister with her left arm and with her right hand clasped my hand firmly. Then we began walking through the treacherous snow, trailing behind the cart. Grandpa was dragging himself along to my right; he clutched my other hand and told me: "Say this, grandson, say it after me." And I said after him: "Exalted and sanctified be His great name…" And the vial of my mother's tears was broken, and her burning tears scorched the snow at our feet. When the cart had gone and the gate was locked again, I no longer saw my father's face, just his smile flickering out from a stack of pain.

In addition to all the other ailments with which Dad was "blessed", he suffered a bout of acute dysentery. The cattle fodder distributed to the camp inmates poisoned his feeble body, which for a long time had been held hostage by diabetes and lung infections. Everything he swallowed was instantly expelled. Mum used to lead him to the latrine in the yard, day and night without respite. They operated this route – Hut 10 to the latrine and back again – as if they had exclusive rights to it. More than once, more than twice, before they even reached the hut, they turned about and retraced their steps, back to the latrine.

Dad bore his suffering heroically, but his lean body withered from day to day. Mum was stubborn in her refusal to compromise with reality, and when the envoys of the sub-conscious came to prepare her for the future, she brushed them aside. With her big body she protected the springs of hope and prevented any attempt to dry them up. Time after time she wrestled with the angel of death who swooped like a ravenous eagle pouncing on his prey, to exact his pound of raddled flesh. Behind his cloak, the colour of the night, he was forever sharpening his hungry cleaver.

"Whatever tricks you get up to, you're not having him!" – she shouted at the angel. Mum stayed awake day and night. She didn't allow herself to sleep at night, because she knew it was a cunning creature she had to deal with, one who would balk at no means to outwit his victims. Usually he appeared under cover of darkness, creeping up from behind, on tiptoe. He would approach till he was just a breath away from his quarry, raise the cleaver, and retreat at once with his spoil.

Mum could detect him from a distance, by smell. The smell

of death struck at every cell in her body and when he came near – from whatever direction – she would spring up to confront him, lashing out with her abrasive tongue and sending him reeling backwards.

"Before you get your claws in him," she told him defiantly, "you'll have to bite off a chunk of my living flesh. Why are you picking on him? Why are you so insistent on taking the life of a man so young? Even Rabbi Feldmann promised him a long life. Can anyone imagine that a fully accredited Jewish rabbi, God's envoy on this earth, would lie?"

The angel of death took two steps back.

When we returned to the hut, Mum was restless. She passed from person to person, asking where Rabbi Feldmann could be found. No one she asked had the faintest idea of his whereabouts. Having finished her first round of questions, Mum didn't give up but immediately launched another round, pestering everyone in the hut – except me. If she'd asked me where I last saw Rabbi Feldmann I'd have told her I saw him quite recently, lying on the cart beside Dad, the cart that two horses were dragging lazily, horses with faces like the face of God.

Two weeks later we again walked behind the cart, this time accompanying Grandpa, who could no longer stand the pain of bereavement and wanted to be reunited with his firstborn son. And I still remembered the words, and although there was no need for this, I said again: "Exalted and sanctified be His great name…"

TWENTY SIX

The prisoners in Hut 10, like the other inmates of the camp, had a dream that they dreamed in chorus both day and night, whether asleep or awake. A dream that had a melodious sound, a fragrant smell, a form fit to swamp the eye, and even a taste to be sensed in the mouth. This was a dream that turned into an anthem, words spoken in the mind or on the lips of the dreamers like a prayer; had this prayer reached the high windows, the sun would have shone above all of them again, the tables in cafes would no longer be segregated, and only real dogs would be denied access to public buildings.

All eyes were lifted to the gate of the camp on the western side, as if this was the eastern wall, through which the dream could enter and leave unmolested, despite the barbed wire surrounding it. Every one of us longed to be on the other side of the gate, to run in the meadows, breathe freedom and harvest liberty in sheaves, like the farmer gathering in his crops from the field. All imagined knocking down the gate, or breaking through it; all had their dream of soaring above it into freedom, like butterflies, despising gates – even those that reach as high as the outskirts of Heaven.

But reality was otherwise. In reality no one broke through the gate and no one flew over it, and those who insisted on passing through it had no option but to go by cart – like the one in which Dad and Grandpa travelled.

"Whose turn will be next?" – Judith asked her brother Tommy.

"All of us," he answered her briefly.

"If our Dad was alive, he'd say it's all in the hands of Heaven," she said.

"It really doesn't matter that much what Dad would have said. What matters is that in Dad's equation, Heaven failed to deliver. The help he was expecting – and he sure knew how to grovel for it – just didn't materialise," he said, unable to restrain his anger.

"And maybe it *did* materialise. Maybe the fact that God called Dad and sent angels to bring him into His presence, was an act of great mercy, to spare him suffering" – Judith tried to placate her brother.

"If those are the kind of mercies you're expecting, sister dear, you can be sure there'll be plenty of them, and new treats for us every day," he replied and turned his back on her, as a sign that the conversation was over; there was nothing more to be said.

Judith wanted to continue the conversation, and although she was well aware of her brother's opinions, she set herself the task of mollifying him, even trying to build a bridge between her faith and Tommy's resolute scepticism.

"What do you reckon, Tommy? Do you think God consults anyone before He takes an important decision?"

Tommy pretended not to hear, and Judith repeated the question.

In the final analysis, Tommy didn't want to hurt his sister, and after a brief pause, he answered her with a question:

"Who do you think God ought to consult?"

"Members of His family perhaps?" she replied hesitantly.

"Judging by the decisions God makes," Tommy responded in a flash – "I'd say He's a confirmed bachelor."

According to the one-way migration of the birds, it seemed that changes of season were in the offing. At the onset of autumn, festival times clustered around the gates of the camp, although the air was not filled – as in former times – with their scents. The new dispensation was not consciously noticed; after all, what artist would have the fevered imagination to draw in his mind's eye the surreal picture of a Jewish New Year celebration in the concentration-camp of Bergen-Belsen? The Germans looked forward to Jewish festivals with undisguised enthusiasm, as these were opportunities to double and treble the number of decrees, which even in normal times were a burden beyond endurance. In the run-up to festivals the Third Reich made a special effort to liberate a double quota of turnips from the emergency stores, tempting a larger proportion of the hungry to opt for death on a full stomach. In General Hund's calendar, the days preceding New Year were dedicated to torments of the mind and the body. Repeated call-outs to the parade ground became routine. Gallows poles multiplied like mushrooms after rain, and on every raised platform stood improvised gibbets, on which the hopes of the Jewish people swung, hiding the horizon so we could no longer see if the sky and the ground were still in contact.

My little sister was impressed by the spectacle, thinking that the gallows were swings. She wanted to have a go too. She tugged at Mum's clothing, asking to be taken on the swings. Mum tried to shut her up, but she went on pleading.

"It's forbidden!" Mum whispered frantically.

"Not true, look, there's uncles swinging there," she protested, and burst into tears.

Luckily for us, General Hund didn't hear my sister weeping, as he was engrossed in one of his favourite pastimes: roll-calls. Every one of us, in order, was supposed to shout in a loud voice: "Jawohl!" When it was the turn of the executed to answer, they maintained a dignified silence. Time after time he called the names of the dead, who proved obdurate. He was enraged by their silence, and as punishment for their disobedience he ordered the flogging of the dead, so that those coming under the shadow of the gallows tree would know – even after death, excruciating torment still awaited them.

On the eve of the Day of Atonement we greeted God with reverence and respect. We were dressed in blue and grey striped prison garments and we listened secretly to the "Kol Nidrei" prayer that emerged simultaneously from all the huts. We did everything to avoid giving an excuse for punishment – on the grounds of "illegal assembly". Everyone sat on his bunk and was a link in the chain of the prayers. Everyone asked pardon and forgiveness for his sins. Everyone with his package of sins, everyone with his own can of worms. The fire of forgiveness, burning away all the sins cast into it, blazed until the small hours of the morning. This was a new kind of "Tashlich" ceremony, Bergen-Belsen style.

I sat hunched up on the second storey, and I had no idea what I was supposed to be casting into the fire. I saw people sitting on their beds with eyes closed and bodies swaying backwards and forwards, as if they could restrain themselves no longer and were about to defecate there and then. And then the thought occurred to me that perhaps I had sinned by peeing on my sister in the night. I was delighted by this revelation, and I thanked God for helping me find a sin I could atone for. And then I asked Him for His help in stopping the phenomenon of nocturnal irrigations, and then I was sad again, realising that if I stopped peeing in the night, I'd no longer have sins to cast into the fire of forgiveness.

The thunder of guns was heard far away. The echo of the falling shells was the most refreshing music imaginable. We sat on our beds with eyes closed, no longer seeing the desolate walls, the mice scurrying from bed to bed, no longer smelling the reek of bodies, the tang of urine and the stench of excrement. The hunt for bed-bugs was suspended and the despair that had been etched at the corners of lean faces – like tattoos

– faded into nothing. We were sitting in a concert-hall, listening to the artillery symphony. The auditorium was packed to overflowing, benches groaning under the weight of clusters of people. If a handful of pins had pleaded to be allowed standing room, they would have been left outside, for lack of space.

The orchestra was in fine fettle. The musicians performed with heavenly virtuosity, as if the survival of all creation rested on their shoulders. The violins wept for joy, the blast of the trumpets nearly blew the roof away, and leading the orchestra and underscoring the sublime melodies were the drums and the cymbals, pounding like a thousand guns.

And as the sounds of thunder grew ever clearer, so the pace of deliverance was quickened.

Two days later we were again loaded into cattle trucks, and Bergen-Belsen was left behind us. The elderly locomotive, as if returning to its youth, began dragging the chain of wagons with revitalised strength, towards an unknown destination. It emerged that the Germans too were endowed with sophisticated musical senses. The sounds of the approaching inferno aroused associations of fire and smoke, and reminded them of the famous German adage: "Time is short and there is much to be done."

The locomotive groaned with the effort, winding between hills and hooting on the plains, encountering a maelstrom of smells. Spring fragrances filtered through the narrow skylights located towards the roofs of the wagons. Our wagon too was infected with the plague of spring, and the scents of blossom percolated into our nostrils.

Someone shouted: "Don't trust them, this is only a dream, they're piping a cocktail of spring smells into the wagons to dope us." Then he asked a friend to pinch him hard and yelped: "Oi, that hurts!" A moment later, all were pinching one another and all were shouting: "Wonderful, it hurts!" A young woman stood by the skylight, tears in her eyes.

"Look at the landscape," she exclaimed with fervour – "it's just like a fashion show, look at the landscape, see how it puts on a shape, and strips it off at once, to put on another." And like a memory returning from a long walk, all sought to be united with the landscape, to touch it from far away, to reach orgasm, if only in the eyes.

Towards evening, the train stopped with a shrieking of brakes. With the benefit of our experience of previous journeys, we knew that cattle convoys didn't stop at intermediate stations, and so all were curious to figure out why we had halted – especially as there was no sign or hint of any station in our field of vision, which stretched away to the horizon, through a full three hundred and sixty degrees. As for the armed guards who accompanied the convoy, whose barking was an inseparable element of the travel experience – it was as if their barking cords had atrophied. It was all very strange. Why had the train stopped in the middle of green fields? To get our nerves on edge? Or were they going to let us out, to stretch our limbs and relieve ourselves? Or did the driver have an assignation with his rustic sweetheart in the bosom of nature?

The meniscus of imagination was overflowing, and before long a stock-exchange of speculations was doing brisk business in our wagon.

Evening descended around us. The fields settled down for the night under a thick quilt of darkness. Not one of us slept. Haunted by waking nightmares we sat in a bubble of fear, and foreboding for the day ahead. Outside, the smells of the night began to stimulate the musical instincts of the crickets, opening up in a noisy chorus that blended with the whistle and the roar of falling shells.

Towards morning, with first light, the door of one of the wagons opened. It was followed by another, and in a matter of moments the doors of all the wagons were opened. Then silence reigned along the whole of the line, as at the time of the Eighteen Benedictions. And the faces of those sitting in the wagons froze, staring motionless at the sight, and mouths struggled to utter a cry that remained trapped deep down in paralysed throats. Only the eyes were free to bathe in the pool of beauty. The vision revealed to us was stunning, like a great fresco that only God is capable of painting, and it can't be touched yet because the paint is still wet. A picture of a slice of intoxicating nature, from the mosaic of creation. Before us rose the hill, that looked from afar like a grand lady, its colourful lower reaches forming the folds of her elegant ball-gown.

No one moved. In dumbstruck amazement we sat on the floor of the wagon, and if God saw us at this time He would surely remember this unique spectacle: cattle trucks turning into a cinema without seats, and the audience watching a film projected by God on a screen of nature.

As we were watching the film, something strange happened. The German guards gathered by the engine, threw away their rifles and in great haste changed out of their uniforms into civilian clothes. Then we heard from outside a monotonous, metallic racket that grew louder from moment to moment. There was no time to guess the source of noise, as just a few seconds later a tank appeared on the brow of the hill overlooking the halted train. Immediately after it came another tank, and when three tanks stood there, someone recognised the emblem of the American Army. Like missiles launched from their silos, all leapt down from the wagons. Silhouettes of people ran up the hill, to kiss the tracks of the tanks and embrace the angels emerging from them. All were beside themselves with joy. The American soldiers, astonished by what they saw, wept like little children, but after the first shock they recovered themselves, leapt down from their tanks and began throwing sweets in all directions. There wasn't a dry spot anywhere; the armour of the tanks and the uniforms of the soldiers were drenched with the tears of the prisoners, whose death-sentence had been commuted to life. The tanks disappeared from view completely, enveloped in humanity. The American soldiers, who had walked in the ways of mortality and survived them, now found themselves almost hugged to death, suffocated by love.

A German soldier who hadn't had time to change out of his uniform was seen fleeing down the slope opposite the hill.

Two Americans on a motor-bike set out in pursuit and caught up with him. And then for the first time I saw a frightened German, raising his hands in surrender and pleading for his life, like a defeated gladiator in the Roman amphitheatre, his fate dependent on the direction of Caesar's thumb.

Mum too climbed to the top of the hill of victory, looking down on the empty train which had stopped a few kilometres short of the furnaces.

"To be liberated on a railway line in the bosom of nature, it's like being born again," she said, holding the two of us close to her big body. While all were celebrating the joy of release on the hill-top, Mum moved aside from the circle of revellers.

Through all the long months of her suffering she had dreamed of this moment, and now she abandoned the crowd to keep her vow. Mum stood in the middle of a flowery field and prayed. From the silent prayer spoken in her heart, only a few words filtered out into the air of the world:

"And here… and now… close… to the chimneys of death… I have given… new life… to my children… and today… this day… my grandchildren too… have been born… to a better life… amen… amen…"

TWENTY SEVEN

If ten measures of freedom descended from Heaven, nine of them landed on our hill. Freedom was laid at our feet and great was the temptation to caress it, but no one touched, lest it be taken away. We were afraid that freedom might yet sprout wings and disappear into the void, before we could take a single bite of it, or worse – it would get snarled up in the tank-tracks and be smashed to pieces.

The hill was now a nucleus of jubilation. A mishmash of voices and tongues drowned the silence of nature. Everyone let off steam, each with his own basket of relief, some speaking to God and some to themselves. A few wept, others laughed, and all the liquids streamed into the lake of tears at the foot of the hill. The survivors gathered into groups, all of them talking at once, in the style of any self-respecting parliament.

"All glory and praise to the American Army!" said someone, and almost the entire crowd burst into loud applause.

"The Messiah!" shouted a religious Jew. "Messiah, Messiah" – the Hassidic contingent echoed, launching at once into an ecstatic Hassidic dance.

A young boy standing on the hillside – reputedly an outstanding *yeshiva* scholar – put both hands to his mouth to form a megaphone, looked up and yelled at the top of his voice, loud enough to be heard in the highest Heaven: "As long as I live I'll never again set foot in Your tabernacle, God, and if You are our father, I'm telling you now I'd rather be an orphan!"

The religious Jew, who had just promised the multitude that the resurrection of the dead was at hand – was stunned into silence.

The sober and cool-headed Tommy Rosenfeld, one of nature's cynics, hugged his sister Judith and whispered in her ear: "What you're looking at, sister dear, is the greatest movie-set crowd scene that God has ever staged. The American soldiers are His actors, and we are the extras. The film will be a hit or a flop – depending on His whim."

My body was among the revellers on the hill, but my thoughts took me back to Hut 10 in Bergen-Belsen, to the night of stars and moon, the first light of Hanukkah. Of course, we had no lights so we celebrated "as if" and "like" and "supposing". Everyone gave free rein to his imprisoned innermost thoughts, wondering what he would do if a second Hanukkah miracle occurred.

Lili Hamer, the beautiful blonde, who was already a young widow when her daughter was born, whose cup of grief had turned to a bottomless well when she lost, one after another,

her parents, her daughter and her younger brother – was not prone to melancholia. The series of cruel disasters that had befallen her would have been enough to drown the strongest of swimmers, but she held her own in the torrents of pain, clutching at a straw of consolation. The dimple that never left her right cheek – even in the darkest of days – was a magnet of hope.

"You know what I'm going to do when we're liberated?" And all eyes turned towards the voice emanating from the darkness of the first light of Hanukkah.

"I'm going to light a big fire in the middle of my lounge and feed it with my worn-out clothes, one piece after another, very slowly. I shall starve the flames until they flare up before me in a dance of entreaty for more and more clothes. And when I've satisfied them I'll light a dozen memorial candles that will never be extinguished and fill the bath with hot water, with little boats of white foam drifting in it, and I'll sit there in the water and sail those boats of foam for seven days and seven nights, till I have cleansed my body from its pollution."

"Before I take a bath I'll have much more important things to do," said Theodore Landau, who in his previous incarnation had weighed 120 kilos. Theodore Landau used to own a haberdashery shop in Debrecen, and his eldest son was in the class below mine in school. Dad used to buy most of his fabrics for tailoring at Theodore's renowned emporium, which had the trade-name of "Elegance."

"My first day of liberty, I'm going to dress up as a hunter, take a couple of assistants and set out on a goose-hunt. We'll raid the farmyards in the suburbs, and I'll hypnotise the fattest geese we find. Then we'll hit the delicatessens in the centre of town and fill our baskets with whole honey-cakes, the size of the Eiffel Tower in Paris. And when we take our seats at the tables for our first regal banquet, beaming joyfully, then the last meal of Louis the Sixteenth before his death will look like a paupers' party in a slum."

I too had dreams that I wanted to fulfil after liberation, but I was too shy to make them public. I told myself that as soon as we were back in our home, I'd go to Theodore Landau's haberdashery shop and buy up his entire stock. I'd spread the materials out on Dad's high cutting-table, and get a two-tier stool to stand on. I'd take his big scissors – although unlike Dad, who used to hold them in one hand, I'd need to use both of mine – then I'd let my tongue hang out and cut out whole kilometres of cloth, working from morning till evening, my tongue wagging – like Dad's – until Mum would say: "Your tongue's had enough of an airing. You can put it away now."

When the Americans transferred us to Hillersleben, a small town not far from the hill of victory and liberation, a new chapter in our lives began. The place was a ghost town, all the residents having fled for fear of the conqueror. The streets were marvellously clean and a veil of calm was stretched over the houses which were built in a semi-rustic style. Window sills were crammed with gaudy flowers, sagging indolently towards the ground.

An average tourist, chancing upon these streets, could easily be deluded into thinking that a flower-market was in progress, operating on a self-service basis – vendors and middlemen having fled to the hills to await quieter times.

The freed of Bergen-Belsen swooped on the town as if finding treasure trove. Strident and hungry they stormed the houses, which capitulated, offering no resistance. The conquest of the houses was accomplished without victims, but the first accounts of liberation were presented for payment not long after the arrival of salvation.

The first victim of freedom was Theodore Landau, who had tried to realise his dream of the morning after liberation. He broke into the house of an aristocratic family, with a larder full of good things. With the help of two volunteers he set about preparing a regal banquet, to which all and sundry of the survivors were invited.

Theodore Landau, who had the most shrivelled stomach of all the diners, after the torments of hunger that he had endured, gorged himself on the tempting, cholesterol-rich delicacies, and once his thirst was quenched and his gut distended, he fell dead before the eyes of all the guests and guzzlers. The geese that he planned to hunt, and the cakes he dreamed of stealing, would just have to wait for another dreamer.

The second night after our liberation, I was assailed by stomach pains. Wave after wave the pangs attacked me, as if I had been chosen as an objective to be taken at any price.

The signals I was picking from the belly zone gave a clear warning that a vicious abdominal war was about to break out. The cries of alarm bursting from my throat shook the concrete walls and judging by first impressions, something in my mother was broken too. To my relief, the mutiny in her heart was rapidly suppressed, and she returned to the role expected of a Messiah in stressful situations.

After all the conventional remedies – such as placing hot saucepan lids on the stomach, and hours of straining over the toilet bowl – had been tried and found wanting, an idea suddenly flashed into her head: "Appendicitis!" she cried, leaping up from her seat as if recoiling from a cluster of snakes. "Please don't let it rupture!" – she pleaded, and ran off to call an army doctor.

Two hours later I was lying on the operating table in the municipal hospital of Haldensleben, a town located seven kilometres from Hillersleben, and a German surgeon of Hungarian extraction was standing over me, brandishing a scalpel.

When I woke up, I saw figures and shapes hovering in the void, as if released from the shackles of the world and the force of gravity. My head was heavy and spinning, and I felt as if a millstone had been placed on my neck.

The army of hovering forms was dressed in the combat gear of hospitals, and every one of them carried a tool-box – the kind used either by heating engineers or surgeons in operating theatres. All the weightless shapes hovering in the void smiled reassuring smiles at me, and yet I felt a sudden stab of fear when I saw the mask of smiles moving on their faces.

When I had recovered from the effects of the anaesthetic and my eyes were fully open, two of the figures were bending over me: my mother and a bespectacled man in white.

"Sweetheart, this is Doctor Heller," she said, tears streaming from her eyes. "We owe him so much, he saved your life" – and her voice was choked with emotion.

All this time, the bespectacled man in white was smiling at me quite unabashed, and Mum withdrew, retreating to the hospital's wall of tears, where she could weep undisturbed.

Every morning, for the next six days, the doctor used to stop by my bedside, pinching my cheek and declaring in a loud voice, for all to hear: "Young man, do you know what a wonderful mother you have?"

The morning of the seventh day, he pulled up a chair and sat beside me, giving me a long look. After a lengthy silence he took my hand and said almost in a whisper: "You know, young man, your mother is an angel from Heaven. It's her you should thank, not me, because she's the one who saved your life. I'll never forget that sight – how she burst into the hospital, carrying you in her arms, crying her eyes out and addressing me in Hungarian: 'Herr Doctor, save him please, he's only just been set free, don't let him die in my arms on the very day of our liberation. Herr Doctor, I'm begging you.'"

Doctor Heller rose from his seat, turned his back to me and took a handkerchief from his pocket. Then he sat down again, as if he had never moved at all, and resumed: "Every day she comes all the way from the town, walking seven kilometres along the railway track, to be with you in the hospital. Every day, on stumbling and swollen feet she's carrying her love over fourteen kilometres, seven here and seven back."

I didn't know what to say to Doctor Heller, and then I had the idea of sticking a pair of angels' wings on him.

TWENTY EIGHT

"Soon we'll be going on a picking-up-the-pieces trip," Mum informed us solemnly. My sister liked the idea of another excursion, while I started looking around for any pieces that needed picking up. When Mum explained to me the concept of "picking up the pieces", I remembered my classmate Miki, who lived in an orphanage and used to visit us for Sabbath meals, at Mum's invitation. Miki grew up like a tree that people had forgotten to water, dependent every day on the charity of Heaven. And if Miki was still alive, I was sure he'd be neither disappointed nor pleasantly surprised; when a traveller has no one to see him off and no one to greet him on his return – it makes no difference to him whether he's coming or going. I wondered if he'd revisit the lake where we left a portion of our childhood behind, and if the swans would remember the bread that he had thrown to them in generous quantities.

One day Mum took us to the big city of Magdeburg. We strolled the streets like people who had emerged from servitude into salvation, like slaves tasting freedom for the first time. We sensed that passers-by were looking at us in the way that one looks at released prisoners, those who suddenly find their long-awaited freedom hard to cope with. There was something strange about our behaviour, which gave us away easily: we walked close to the walls in single file, afraid to spread out across the pavement lest we encounter any of our former oppressors, creeping out of their hiding-places to pounce on the unwary. Our heads were still hunched between our shoulders, backs bowed and eyes darting around suspiciously in all directions. Suddenly we heard barking behind us, and the three of us started, terrified. Mum instinctively spread her big wings above us, and when we turned we saw a little poodle, yapping at us quite affably. But we still looked around anxiously for the dog's armed companion.

Magdeburg was licking its wounds. There wasn't a single street without open wounds, and the fresh signs of bombardment were visible every step of the way. In addition to this, the city itself had a doleful and resentful air, as if it was covered by layer upon layer of dark depression. Despite the best efforts of a spring sun, the streets seemed to be bathed in the gloom of perpetual twilight.

We stood before the half-empty display window of a food shop. As I stared at the meagre stock of delicacies, the taste-glands in my mouth coming back to life and my saliva flowing, the reflection of a familiar face appeared on the pane of glass. When I identified the man behind the face, I panicked and without turning round I tugged at Mum's dress. Mum needed no time at all to be sure that it was the face of one of General Hund's trusted henchmen that was visible in the window. She was determined to have the criminal arrested, and was wondering how this could be put into effect, in an unfriendly environment and without a single man on hand to help her. When our eyes crossed in the shop window, the German recognised us at once, and could read my mother's thoughts.

A moment later there were only three reflections in the window. The "superior human being" disappeared if the earth had swallowed him. Presumably he had gone underground.

The aimless strolling, and the futile attempt to catch a Nazi criminal exhausted us. We sat down on a heap of rubble in the shadow of a bombed-out building, that had collapsed like a house of cards. Mum was bitterly disappointed, acutely aware of a missed opportunity. I asked her if God protected Nazi criminals and she didn't answer. What surprised me was the fact that for once she didn't rebuke me, as she always used to, for challenging the ways of God.

Worn out, the three of us fell asleep, sprawled on a mattress of stones and too exhausted to notice the protest demonstration mounted by a dozen or so mice. The mice scurried over our recumbent bodies as if they were sole proprietors of the ruined property and felt threatened by our incursion.

I was the first to wake up, and at once I sensed a vile stench, assaulting my nostrils in waves. The stronger the stink became, the more strangely familiar it seemed to me. It woke Mum up too. "I know that smell," she said. Before we had time for another thought, standing there in front of us was the legendary Miki, with his full panoply of familiar aromas. Mum was overjoyed, clasping him tightly to her bosom. Miki was moved as well, as if finding a treasure he'd been seeking for ages.

The lean youth had grown up a lot since we last saw him. In the interim, it seemed that every number he'd gambled on in the roulette of life had come up; he'd have been barred from all the casinos in the world. Miki was naturally shy and reticent, and it took a lot of patience, and subtle inducements, to coax an account of his experiences out of him, experiences buried deep in the recesses of the belly and the psyche.

When the Jews from the ghettoes were assembled in the brick factory, Miki decided, wisely as it turned out, to slip away from the other inmates of the orphanage. An only child, he naturally sought out the company of adults. An instinct for survival guided him towards a narrow patch of floor close to a middle-aged, childless couple, and here he took up residence. When the people were loaded on the train, Miki boarded as the "son" of the couple, who agreed to be his "parents". When the train reached Austria and the Germans opened the doors of the wagon, they found that Miki's "mother" had died on the way. She suffered from an acute heart condition and during the agonising journey by cattle-truck, starved of oxygen, she choked to death and gave her soul back to whoever had given it to her, with a none too generous hand.

His "father" was bound to him with firm bonds of affection, and he promised to give him his name once the nightmare was over. In Bergen-Belsen Miki fell victim to a severe bout of dysentery, his stomach refusing to tolerate the cattle-fodder served twice a day. His "father" took his own life in his hands, determined to rescue his "son" from the clutches of death. He managed to obtain a supply of clean water, instead of the contaminated liquid that the prisoners were expected to drink, and seeing Miki crossing the threshold, back into life, he hummed wordless hymns of thanksgiving.

When British soldiers broke down the gates of the camp, they found Miki's father dangling from the gallows. The Germans had succeeded in hanging him just in time, a day before liberation.

That day of rescue and liberation, Miki became an orphan again.

Survivors of the camps swooped on any vehicles travelling in the direction of home. Carts laden with refugees, hitched to hungry horses, straggled along the roads. Trains were in operation too, crammed to capacity and moving on tracks which, after a long intermission, were once again available to two-way traffic. In those times, there was no such thing as a timetable. The carriages, coupled to engines of pensionable age, were virtually invisible, masked by the hordes of people climbing on the roofs and clinging to the sides like clusters of grapes. In normal times, sitting on the roof of a moving train, with tunnels in the offing, would not be considered an efficient or confidence-building mode of transport, but from the perspective of the roof-travellers, all this was child's play compared with the perils they had faced in the recent past.

Among the lucky passengers, luckiest of all were those with seats inside the carriages, sandwich-style.

We were lucky too. We boarded such a train and through Mum's resourcefulness we were admitted to the family of sardines. The trick was to find a space and hold it against all comers. It took determination and unshakable self-confidence to keep one's property. Any hesitation or indecision, and your place was liable to be forfeited, however noisy your protests.

Between Mum and me my sister sat, and to my left a young man had squeezed in. Miki, who had joined our truncated family, sat opposite. The train trundled along lazily, not needing stations as an excuse to stop. It spent more time standing still than in motion. Considering the antiquity of the locomotive, the fact that the train was moving at all was something for the record-books.

"Don't you dare touch my son!" – Mum exclaimed with a sudden flash of anger, landing a firm slap on the right hand of the man beside me, a hand moving sinuously in the direction of my trouser-buttons.

"But I didn't notice," the man protested, his plot foiled and his indignation overflowing, to no avail: "I think my hand went to sleep and moved towards your son's belt, without any intention on my part."

"Don't get clever with me, young man," Mum retorted, still seething. "Any more of that and I'll have you arrested."

The youth realised at once the kind of person he was up against, and he roused his "sleeping" hand and beat a hasty retreat, his tail between his legs.

Suddenly I had room to stretch on the seat, and I remembered the red-haired, bespectacled and bearded man, on another train, who liked children and instead of stroking their heads, stroked their willies – mine too.

Now that it had happened to me for the second time, I found the whole business puzzling and disconcerting as well and I decided to ask Mum's advice.

"Tell me please, Mum," – I turned to her cautiously – "when I grow up, if I like children, am I supposed to stroke their willies instead of their heads?"

Mum's eyes were closed and she pretended not to hear. Or perhaps she really was asleep, after her decisive victory over the man who had been exiled, shame-faced, from the carriage.

TWENTY NINE

Days later and after a tortuous journey, the train arrived at the gates of Debrecen, panting heavily and nearly falling off the rails for weariness. When it stopped in the city's main railway station, it seemed the engine was on the point of expiring.

Mum was very agitated and impatient. She embraced us warmly and kept hold of us a long time. When we alighted from the train, a smiling woman stopped beside us, and turning to Mum, said to her: "You know, lady, your two children are like a pair of flowers." And Mum watered the flowers with her tears. She put her head close to mine, and in a whirl of emotions whispered to me: "Go on, dear, run to Grandma's house, quick. Go and see if my sister and my mother are alive, if they're still there. If you find them alive, tell Aunt Elizabeth she can add three more names to the list of the living. Get going, lad, we'll be right behind you."

And I began running with head erect and chest inflated, my feet hitting the ground at a steady pace. My running was proud, as if I was one of the Olympic torch-bearers. I wanted them all to see my triumphant run – not like the time before, when they saw me running in panic. I had wings of white feathers, like in a dream.

The looks of those around me gave everything away: I saw eyes blazing with hate, eyes open wide in disbelief, and I also saw a pair of eyes shedding tears. And already I was hovering in the air, feet barely touching the ground and my right fist clenched as if holding a torch… and then I heard the echo of running feet behind me, and when I turned back I saw Willy closing on me, signalling to me with his eyes: "We're going to show them yet, we're going to show them!"

When he caught up with me, he held out a hand of brotherly affection and began intoning his famous song in my ear: "Tommy Langer is a fool, clowns around all day in school…" At that very moment who should pop out from a side-alley but Tommy the *Langer*, smiling from ear to ear, and running on he laid at Willy's door a small garland of thorns from the seminary of the cynics: "Hey, pal, when are you going to learn the tune and stop spoiling it?" I howled with mirth. In the crowd sounds of wonderment were heard: it didn't seem reasonable that a prestigious runner like myself should be almost choking with laughter while the race was in progress.

When I reached the neighbourhood grocery shop, I saw Isaac Rosenfeld loading a basketful of provisions on the back of an elderly Jew, and having parted from him and wished him good health, he took from his drawer the "Charged to God" account-book and wrote something in it. His hand smoothed down his white beard and his lips were seen murmuring:

"Thank you, God."

Spring was in the air, and a following wind helped my progress.

As I sped on down the high street, I noticed from a distance a big gathering outside Yonah Adler's shoe shop. As I approached, I found myself in an awards ceremony, honouring the town's most courteous commercial enterprise. I saw hundreds of contented customers emerging from the shop carrying shoe-boxes tied with colourful smiling ribbons. I looked up at the two tall towers of the Protestant church. They seemed shorter than they had been before; perhaps they were bowing their heads in shame.

From there I turned towards my school. I burst through the gates and without hesitation went running and skipping to the upper floor. I entered the classroom in mid-lesson. I wanted to retreat, but it was too late; I was caught on the hook of my teacher and *bete noire* Mister Schwartzkopf, who put down the chalk he was holding, adjusted the glasses perched on his nose, and said in his honeysweet voice: "Good morning, Elijah. What happened this morning, did the cock forget to crow? You see, boys, another zero- squared who can't get up on time." And all the flood-gates in the classroom were breached, swamping the pupils with a tidal wave of laughter.

Now I couldn't remember where I'd left the glue, due for its rendezvous with the maths teacher's bum.

I was the prisoner of my lower limbs. Of all the many parts of my body, my legs were in control. They led me to the courtyard of the synagogue, not far from the school. When

I arrived there, I ran around the yard in circles, then sat on a bench to rest awhile and travel to the furthest extremes of memory. The windows of the sanctuary were open and sounds of singing filtered into the yard, caressing the spirits. A Sabbath fragrance rose in my nostrils, and I found myself in the middle of a broad circle, with my longings hemming me in and dancing around me the dance of nostalgia. Then a second circle was formed, a third and even a fourth, until the whole yard was filled with rings of dancers, arm-in-arm, clinging to one another like links in a chain. And rising in the middle the voice of the ruddy-faced cantor, Samuel Braun, singing anthems in honour of the Sabbath: "Come, my love, to greet the bride, let us greet the Sabbath," and all the dancers – some ten thousand bridegrooms, and I among them, a bridegroom too, one of the host.

I had to struggle to make my way out of the crowd. Without realising it, I quickened the pace of my running. The many passers-by who had gathered by the roadside reckoned they were witnessing a mirage, a *fata morgana*: how could I be running through the central streets of their beautiful city, when I was supposed to be somewhere else entirely? Something in their innermost hearts was broken. They always believed the German people a people of honour. Every Hungarian sucked in his admiration for the Germans with his mother's milk and no one had the slightest doubt: a German promise would definitely be kept.

When they saw me hovering, striking the pose of a victor, cracks appeared in their blind admiration. Gradually it dawned on them that a German promise was in fact a bouncing cheque, and the German people nothing other than a bunch of liars. I was swamped with happiness that penetrated to the very last cell of my body.

Along the route I recognised ruffians from the "Crossbow" gangs, who had often assaulted us in the past and were always at the spearhead of violence. Now they stood in the second or third rank, hands in pockets, hunched and silent, as if they had swallowed their tongues.

Suddenly, a velvety female voice caressed my neck. I turned round and saw sparks of beauty twinkling in the air. Olga stood in the doorway of the "Style" boutique, hands outstretched, lovelier than ever and statuesque as a model, dressed with elegance and daring, a deep décolletage exposing her breasts. I ran to meet her, to find shelter in her arms. She pressed my head to her bosom and wept for joy, as if given back something precious and long lost. Her eyes were two dripping taps that someone forgot to turn off. I was so agitated and emotional my throat clammed up and I could only stammer breathlessly:

"O-O-Olga....you, you'll... c-c-catch a c-c-cold... and p-p-people can s-s-see your t-t-titties..."

"Good luck to them," she replied: "It sharpens the eyesight and improves concentration."

It began to rain. I looked up and saw two little clouds pissing in an arc. It seemed the angels had fallen asleep and forgotten to start them on time.

The "Golden Bull" hotel hadn't changed at all: it looked like someone who still had sap in his loins, unpainted, undecorated, as if time had stood still, like a man marooned in middle age. As if the years had taken a break, stopped to rest awhile.

Table 10 was covered with green baize, as before. The regular group sat around the table, its composition almost unchanged. Someone else was sitting in my father's chair, someone I didn't recognise. Robbie Friedmann saw me the moment I entered the smoke-filled monastery of cards. He was in high spirits and he even winked at me mischievously. On the other hand, the new "victim" had broken out into a cold sweat, his nose was stuck into his cards and he gave the impression that the only option left to him – in view of the cards Robbie had dealt him – was to write a will.

Robbie gestured to me to approach the window, that was once my regular vantage-point, looking out from the temple of the cards to the world outside. Nothing had changed since then: the same taxis and the same drivers, waiting in line, as before, for the same passengers.

Through the window I saw a figure pacing about at the front of the theatre, and it was only then that Robbie Friedmann's signals took on meaning and significance. I slid down the banister of the internal stairs of the three storey building, brushed past the concierge and rushed out into the street as if my trousers were on fire. I had to cross the street from side to side, and suddenly I collided with a small woman who was hurrying to catch the tram. Kitty stood facing me, alarmed and embarrassed by the unexpected encounter. When she'd regained some composure she put her hand to her heart and said to me in her most sanctimonious voice: "I'm not to blame, I swear I'm not to blame, there's nothing left, the Germans took everything." And without another word she turned and ran, jumped on a moving tram and disappeared among the passengers.

Dad stood in the foyer of the theatre, holding two tickets.

"You're almost too late," he said.

"I was at the 'Golden Bull,'" I explained.

"What's this, have you taken up playing cards?"

"What would I want with cards, Dad? I was looking for you."

"You've forgotten already?" – as usual, he left the question hanging in the air.

"Forgotten what, Dad?" I asked curiously.

"You've forgotten we agreed to meet at the theatre at four o'clock after the war?"

I was ashamed.

When we sat in the auditorium, and Dad's big curtain was raised from the stage, it was only then it occurred to me: Dad had given up his beloved card-game, for me.

After the show we sat in a carriage and travelled by a new, unconventional route. Dad preached me a heart-stirring sermon… with his eyes. And I tuned all my receiving stations to all wavelengths, to take in his broadcast. Dad went on transmitting and it seemed to me I heard music.

When the carriage passed by Pitzi Kleinmann's "house", the windows were closed and sealed from the inside with dark curtains. This was the sign meaning that the great maestro was not to be disturbed: he was dealing with an important "client", or this was Fitzi's dream time, when he dreamed of carnal dalliance with his "beloved" – Eva Waldmann.

Dad stared long and hard at the clairvoyant's house, and asked the driver to stop the carriage, but then he changed his mind and told him to drive on to the big wood.

At the approaches to the big wood I stepped down from the carriage and Dad signalled to the driver to carry on. The driver whipped his horses into a gallop, which wasn't his usual practice, and the carriage sped away, winding among the trees until it disappeared from sight.

I didn't see my Dad again. I firmly believed that he had turned into a big tree in the forest, with a shady and sheltering canopy. As time passed I made it a habit to return to the big wood and visit a certain oak. And when I embraced the oak, it was like embracing my Dad.

I continued my solitary run, my objective being the lake of the swans. I passed by many trees in the wood and suddenly the lake appeared in all its glory. Someone stood by the jetty, constantly glancing at his watch. Two bulging bags hung on his shoulders, swinging back and forth. It was Miki, waiting for me, with a generous supply of breadcrumbs. I approached him, stopped running, and we fell into each other's arms. Even as we embraced, there was a big surprise awaiting us. All the swans came up from the water to the shore, pacing the full length of the jetty with wings entwined, black and white together and then, as a final touch of magic, from out of the depths of the lake rose a little girl – the girl with the golden curls emerged from the water and like a happy frog sprang into our outstretched arms. "I knew we'd meet again," she said, and the surface of the lake rose by a centimetre at least.

When I burst into the house where Grandma and Aunt Elizabeth lived, my mother and my sister were already there. "We were worried about you," she said. "How is it that you left the station before us, and you've only just got here?"

And I looked into the mirror, and hardly recognised my face, where the first bristles of a beard were beginning to show.

CPSIA information can be obtained
at www.ICGtesting.com
Printed in the USA
BVHW041814131222
654139BV00001B/7